THE
BAPTIST
WAY

THE
BAPTIST
WAY

DISTINCTIVES
OF A
BAPTIST CHURCH

R. STANTON NORMAN

ACADEMIC

NASHVILLE, TENNESSEE

ISBN: 978–0–8054–3152–0

Published by B&H Publishing Group
Nashville, Tennessee

Dewey Decimal Classification: 230.6
Subject Heading: BAPTISTS—DOCTRINES

12 13 14 15 16   22 21 20 19 18

DEDICATION

To my loving wife Joy
*"Many daughters have done nobly,
but you excel them all."*

CONTENTS

PREFACE

The more I write, the more I am convinced that every book is a collaborative effort, and this book is no exception. The person of foremost acknowledgment is my wife Joy, to whom this book is lovingly dedicated. She is my greatest encourager and advocate, and even more, she is my best friend. After twenty-one years of marriage, I still marvel that our gracious God would bestow upon me the privilege and blessing of sharing our lives together. If ever a wife embodied the qualities of a "gentle and quiet spirit" that exemplify a godly woman, Joy surely does. Her love and sacrifice for our family are boundless. Her grace and dignity honor our Lord. Her life radiates the fruit of the Spirit. She believes in me and my ministry more than I do. I am truly a blessed man.

I also want to acknowledge the contribution of my three sons, Andrew, Daniel, and Stephen. I have no greater joy than being their father. This book was produced in the midst of all the stuff that goes with being a dad. I truly marvel as I watch our heavenly Father shape and grow these guys into three of the finest young men a father could ever hope to have. Their patience with me as I cloistered away to write this book far exceeded their years. I am deeply grateful for the sacrifice of time and attention they made in order for this work to see the light of day.

Several persons who serve with me in Southern Baptist denominational life also deserve special mention. I want to express my appreciation to my president, Charles S. Kelley, my provost, Steve W. Lemke, and the trustees of the New Orleans Baptist Theological Seminary. My gratitude for the conferral of a sabbatical leave made this project possible. The encouragement and support of my president and provost for my various writing and professional projects cannot be overstated.

I am fortunate to have colleagues who believe in me and support my passionate pursuits. My dean and friend, Jerry Barlow, is a source of immeasurable encouragement. I am grateful for his support in this endeavor. The members of the Theological and Historical division of the seminary also merit recognition. They are Daniel Holcomb, Robert Stewart, Ken Keathley, Lloyd Harsch, and Jeff Riley. These men add to the joy of my teaching ministry at New Orleans Baptist Theological Seminary. I am most appreciative of the collegiality and friendship that we share.

I also want to thank my new friend and colleague, Ed Stetzer, who currently serves with the North American Mission Board as the director of the Church Planting Institute. Our recent conversations and collaborations on the "Ecclesiological Guidelines to Inform Southern Baptist Church Planters" helped stimulate and clarify my thinking on some of the crucial issues discussed in this book. In addition, I want to express my appreciation to Bart D. Box, who serves as fellow for the Baptist Center for Theology and Ministry at New Orleans Seminary. His research and editorial assistance proved invaluable in this project. Gratitude is also extended to Jason Sampler, who graciously compiled the indexes.

I also want to give special acknowledgment to John Landers of Broadman & Holman Publishers. This book would not have been possible without his encouragement and support. His assuring yet firm editorial supervision pushed this project to its completion.

This book is a labor of love for Southern Baptists, and I am honored to give my life in service to them. I hope this work will strengthen our resolve to be true to those doctrinal convictions that have been and remain unique to Baptists. I also pray that our theological distinctives will undergird our churches in their kingdom witness and work. May the Lord bless the people called Baptists as we willingly submit to his lordship and obediently submit to his Word.

INTRODUCTION

"The silence is deafening." This well-worn adage aptly describes the dearth of writings on the subject of Baptist distinctives and Baptist theology. Relatively few recent works have tried to "fill the silence." A great need exists for a contemporary restatement of those doctrines that constitute the distinctive theological identity of Baptists.

CONTEMPORARY CHALLENGES TO OUR BAPTIST DISTINCTIVES

This need is clearly reflected within the Southern Baptist Convention. Most of the works published lately that speak to the issue of Baptist distinctives typically reflect a "moderate" Baptist persuasion. In my estimation, these works reflect a concerted effort to redefine Baptist distinctives from a skewed, prejudicial theological bias. If Southern Baptists are not vigilant, our silence on this issue will concede our Baptist heritage to those who desire to redefine our historic Baptist identity. If left unanswered, these attempts could eventually make theological inroads into our Southern Baptist churches. We must answer these moderate restatements with deliberate and thoughtful affirmations that are biblically, historically, and theologically accurate.

In addition to the need to answer the attempts to redefine Baptist identity, I believe we are witnessing a steady erosion of "doing church" from a Baptist perspective. For example, there exists in Southern Baptist life an informal culture in which successful ministries are measured by the growth and size of the church. In other words, the value of a ministry is determined by the pace of numerical growth or the dramatic size of the institution. Because of this mentality, anything that threatens the growth or size of the church may potentially be eliminated. Sadly, a thoroughgoing commitment to certain theological convictions is perceived by some as a barrier to growth.

This "growth at any costs" mentality has led some Baptist leaders and churches to jettison the core tenets of our Baptist identity, regarding them as outdated, irrelevant, or detrimental to the growth of a church. If doctrinal convictions are allowed to shape the faith and practice of our churches (so the thinking goes), then church growth will be impeded, thereby conveying the impression of an ungodly or unsuccessful ministry. In order to meet this superficial criterion, some people in Southern Baptist life are willing to sacrifice our distinctive, doctrinal convictions on the altar of success.

Although the need to reach more people is commendable, we do not achieve meaningful growth by compromising our convictions. The abandonment of theological convictions will devastate the vitality and mission of our churches. The lack of emphasis on doctrine, which is supposed to improve the growth of a church, will in fact result in the ultimate demise of the church.

For example, if we fail to maintain a staunch commitment to the doctrine of a regenerate church membership, we will build an ecclesiastical structure that will permit (if not encourage) the inclusion of unbelievers as church members. (I actually know of some churches that are doing this!) This "church" becomes an unholy organization of unbelievers in which the Spirit of God will not dwell, and it will lose its power and integrity in any witness and work that it might undertake.

An organization can experience numerical growth and have a dynamic, institutional culture, but the absence of biblical beliefs and practices disqualifies that organization as a New Testament church. The philosophy that was supposed to enhance church growth actually undermines the very purpose for which it was adopted.

Another deplorable development that challenges the distinctive theological identity of our Baptist churches is the potential influx of theological pluralism. With the growing definition of "theological tolerance" as "theological affirmation and validation," our Baptist churches are constantly challenged to maintain their unique doctrinal convictions.

The statement of Reverend Dr. Jessup, moderator of the Presbyterian General Assembly, to a gathering of Baptists a century ago echoes loudly and clearly to the Baptists of today: "What reason is there for the separate and unique existence of Baptists?" If Baptists today do not intentionally and consistently restate our Baptist distinctives, our unique theological identity may be lost in the swell of this rampant ideological pluralism. Should Baptists capitulate to the spirit of a convictionless tolerance, we will lose a theological identity that has guided our Baptist churches in their mission since our beginning. Our Baptist identity would simply be absorbed into the amorphous pluralism of our day.

We must guard against losing our "Baptist identity." Our distinctive beliefs do matter. They are the convictions that, in great measure, determine the life and mission of our Baptist churches. If we lose our distinctive identity, the word *Baptist* will become a vacuous concept designating nothing more than a certain building located at a certain place.

Another justification for a restatement of our Baptist distinctives was impressed upon me several years ago at a professional meeting. Each year New Orleans Baptist Theological Seminary, where I currently serve on the faculty, sponsors an endowed lectureship in which a faculty member is selected to make a scholarly presentation on a topic of significant interest. The subject of the presentation for this particular year was church health. The professor selected that year began his presentation by posing the provocative question, "How do we define a 'healthy church'?" Following this inquiry, my friend began an in-depth, critical description and assessment of the various and complex proposals for defining church health. His fascinating presentation, coupled with his candid admission that he had not yet developed a satisfactory model, stimulated my interest in the subject. How would I define a healthy church?

My friend's presentation intrigued me on two levels. First, the amount of research developed in this field was immense and diverse. I learned that church health is a transcendent concern. We as Southern Baptists are not the only denomination asking, "What is a healthy church?" Christians of all nationalities and in most denominations are equally interested in this subject.

Second, most of the answers given to this important question tend to be statistical assessments. The studies on church health presented that day addressed the issue primarily in quantitative terms; that is, church health is often assessed numerically, such as the size of the congregation, average attendance in worship or Bible study, number and size of ministries staffed or supported by the church, and numbers of additions or baptisms. Although church health often is measured by statistical categories, I believe church health should be theologically formulated before statistical analysis begins.

As I listened to my colleague's fine presentation, I could not help but recast the subject theologically. I readily admit that, as a theologian, I think in theological categories, and I recognize that my perspective is biased toward my passion and discipline. Yet I am nonetheless convinced that church health is basically a theological concern. Statistical analysis is certainly needed for the correct assessment of numerical data. The information gleaned from statistical examinations is crucial for identifying trends or patterns, as well as isolating relational factors and behaviors that are legitimate dynamics of church health. But statistical analysis alone cannot define those beliefs that characterize church health. Statistics can measure and identify, but they cannot describe the convictions or practices that constitute church health.

In addition, most definitions of church health that are determined primarily by statistical measurements tend to assume a certain definition of a church. That is, the "health" part is the focus, and the "church" part is assumed. The assumption of a singular definition of "church," however, may be unfounded. If we cannot establish what a church is, how do we know if a church is healthy or sick?

Further, differing denominations understandably approach the task of defining church health differently. Certain convictions and qualities about a Christian church do transcend denominational boundaries. Because each Christian denomination has beliefs and practices unique to its own confessional tradition, definitions of church health typically include both those elements that transcend confessional traditions and the distinctive theological tenets of each denomination. We should recognize that any definition of church health will be peculiar to the confessional tradition in which it was developed. Because of denominational differences, the task of developing a transdenominational definition of church health may be elusive.

We are not the only generation of Christians to grapple with issues like these. Our Baptist forefathers also struggled with similar questions. For them, however, the question was not so much, "What is a healthy church?" but rather, "What is a church?" and in particular, "What is a New Testament church?" The distinctive identity of Baptists actually arose as these believers attempted to have churches that were faithful to what they believed was taught in the New Testament.

These early Baptists struggled to define the faith and practice of a "true" church or, as they were fond of saying, a "New Testament church." As our Baptist ancestors articulated and practiced what would become our distinctive theological identity, they were in fact defining what they believed to be a New Testament church. For them, a church founded upon and committed to the teachings of the New Testament was a healthy church. To use our vernacular, they wanted to have "healthy churches." The result was Baptist churches.

We as Baptists believe that our distinctive theological identity contributes significantly to the health of our churches. Our Baptist distinctives are not the only traits that define church health, but we do believe that they are essential components of a healthy church. This conviction was true for our Baptist ancestors, and the same conviction should characterize Baptists today. The distinctive doctrines of Baptists are actually the theological traits that define and shape our churches. I fully believe that, ideally, a healthy church is a Baptist church.

THE IMPORTANCE OF BAPTIST DISTINCTIVES

Some Baptists try to downplay or diminish our theological distinctives. In fact, some go so far as to suggest that our views on congregational polity or the mode of baptism are the only factors that distinguish us from the rest of Christendom. Although these ecclesiastic traits are true of Baptists, they do not fully account for the distinction of Baptists from other denominations. I readily admit that a majority of our distinctive convictions are most visibly expressed in our churches. Our unique convictions, however, also impinge upon matters of salvation (age of accountability, regenerate church membership, individual accountability to God) and religious authority (complete submission to the New Testament for faith and practice). Our Baptist distinctives thus illustrate the organic, interrelationship of our beliefs.

Other Christians relegate our emphasis on our unique convictions to an outdated intransigence—a theological stubbornness that is incompatible with our tolerant, pluralistic age. In response to this charge, we must remember that all Christian denominations have theological convictions that serve as the fundamental foundation for the faith and practice of their churches.

For example, the inability of sixteenth-century Lutherans and Calvinists to agree on the mode of the Lord's presence in the Communion elements may appear to some people as insignificant unless we are aware of the Christology underlying the viewpoints of each position. In this regard, our Baptist distinctives are no different than those distinctives of other denominations. Our unique convictions are rooted in certain theological beliefs that determine our understanding for the faith and practice of our churches. We believe our distinctive tenets are the result of a well-grounded biblical, theological reasoning. When perceived in this light, our emphasis on our distinctives is no different from similar emphases of other Christian denominations.

I contend, as do most Baptists, that our theological distinctives are our attempt to hear and obey the voice of our Lord Jesus Christ as he speaks to the church through the New Testament. Baptists strive to be Bible-believing Christians who glorify God in everything we do. We believe that glory is brought to God as our churches fulfill the mandates entrusted to them—mandates that include the command of Christ to observe everything that he has commanded us (Matt. 28:19). Our distinctive identity is in part our obedient response to this command.

Our Baptist distinctives also represent our attempt to follow consistently the implications of the New Testament for the church and its mission. We believe that God the Father issues the call of salvation through the Holy Spirit. Our understanding of this truth in all its intricacies determines our relationship and submission to Christ, the nature and mission of the church, the meaning of the ordinances, the right governance of the church, and the purpose of religious liberty.

As Baptists we assume a responsibility to be faithful to our theological heritage and to express our distinctive convictions in our local Baptist congregations. Every Baptist is responsible to know the Baptist confessional tradition that shapes the nature and ministry of our churches. Our Baptist beliefs constitute the standard of association for those churches which choose to join together for various ministry endeavors. Baptists must learn to appreciate anew the unique identity forged by those who discovered and refined these tenets. To misrepresent or modify the tenets that historically have distinguished the Baptists is to belittle the labor and sacrifice of those who have preceded us. In addition, to redefine the essence of our Baptist identity destroys the foundation of the association of our Baptist churches.

INTENTIONS AND ASSUMPTIONS

This project is actually the next phase of my work in Baptist distinctives. In my previous book, *More Than Just a Name: Preserving Our Baptist Identity*, I provided a historical examination of the development and nature of writings on Baptist distinctives. I noted that Baptists do have a confessional identity and that our distinctive theological traits constitute the "Baptist side" of that identity. In addition, I stipulated that Baptists have a unique theological method inherent in writings on Baptist distinctives. I also traced the development of two distinctive traditions in Southern Baptist life.

The present work is an attempt to identify and describe the distinctive traits of Baptists and thus is more prescriptive than descriptive in nature. I recognize that there is great diversity in the Baptist family on many issues, yet I believe there are certain traits that make us Baptist. I also believe these doctrinal tenets have served as a means of identifying and evaluating those churches that are truly Baptist and, from our perspective, most faithful to the teachings of the New Testament.

Not all Baptists agree with the specific theological conceps identified in this book as "Baptist distinctives." My own conviction is that the concepts identified in this book are faithful to the historical and theological evidence. Building on the evidence examined and the categories established in *More Than Just a Name*, my intent in this book is to elaborate on those theological tenets that are distinctive of the Reformation tradition of Baptist distinctives. This book seeks to restate those emphases that have characterized Baptists throughout their history. But this work has certain limitations.

First, this is not a full-fledged ecclesiology. That project may be pursued down the road, but this book is not it. Certain aspects of church life are omitted simply because they do not classify as a Baptist distinctive. The focus of this study is primarily on those theological tenets that have been classically regarded as our Baptist distinctives. I do include one short chapter that addresses issues not typically regarded as part of our distinctive convictions. The inclusion of this material, however, is primarily to help fill in some of the gaps of discussions in previous chapters.

Second, I will treat theological concerns seriously, yet my intent is to keep the discussion as nontechnical as possible. I am writing for the church, not the academy. In this sense, this book is more of a primer on Baptist distinctives than an in-depth analysis.

Third, this book is primarily directed toward my own denomination, the Southern Baptist Convention. My hope is that other Baptists will read and profit from this study. My target audience, however, is my own denomination. My prayer is that this work can serve as a sourcebook that will assist our Southern Baptist churches in their task of being the people of God in the twenty-first century.

Chapter 1

BIBLICAL AUTHORITY

The Baptist story is one of a group of believers who desired to have churches based on the authority of the New Testament. These kinds of churches required a certain belief about and commitment to biblical authority. Baptists originated as a people who were unswervingly dedicated to the belief that the Bible is the authoritative, written revelation of God. The Scriptures served as the foundation for our Baptist ancestors on which they built New Testament churches.

In their distinctive and other theological writings, Baptists have always traced their origin and existence to the prominent place they give to the Bible for their faith and practice. Baptists do not adhere to a belief of biblical inspiration that formally differs from other Christian denominations. In other words, there is not a "Baptist view" of how the Bible came to be or a "Baptist view" of biblical authority. But Baptists do argue that our consistent and absolute adherence to biblical authority is different from non-Baptist Christians.

Baptists insist that our consistent and exclusive adherence to the Scriptures for matters of faith and practice distinguishes us from other Christians. Baptists further contend and often strive to prove that other Christian denominations elevate other types of religious expression to the same level as the Bible. Baptists assert that any perspective, practice, experience, or tradition that does not have biblical support or is not subordinated to biblical authority must be rejected.

SOURCES FOR RELIGIOUS AUTHORITY

Non-Christians and many Christians have always and still do regard traditions, philosophies, experiences, or other realities as viable sources for religious authority. In the following discussion, I will briefly identify and critique these other sources of religious authority. I will then examine the Baptist conviction about biblical authority and the prominent place of the New Testament in shaping our faith and practice.

THE CHURCH AS THE SOURCE OF RELIGIOUS AUTHORITY

The Roman Catholic Church states that Jesus Christ founded a visible society to which he gave his truth in the form of Scripture and tradition. The Catholic Church further affirms that Christ empowered that society to rule itself by the bishopric and to interpret the revelation of Scripture and tradition to all Christians. The Roman Catholic Church claims that it is the sole society in which the rights of biblical and theological interpretation are vested. The Roman Catholic Church teaches that it neither adds to existing revelation nor receives new revelation. Although the church claims that it does not discover new truth, it does make explicit what is implicit within the revelatory tradition.[1]

Rome claims to have an interpretation of the written revelation in its tradition carried on within the church as secret, unwritten, and apostolic. The church, as God's representative on earth, maintains that it is infallible in its interpretation of the written revelation. Therefore, when the church speaks, it speaks with the same authority as if the Lord himself were speaking. The church controls all definitions of truth, and all doctrinal formulations have been delegated to the apostles and their successors. In addition, the Roman Catholic Church bestows great authority upon church councils, creeds, and the writings of church fathers.[2]

Baptists reject this particular understanding of religious authority. We typically agree that the early church lived in submission to the Old Testament and apostolic teaching. But the completion of the New Testament as the apostolic witness and revelation to Jesus Christ abrogated any reliance on any traditions or teachings not contained within the canon.[3]

Baptists recognize that we do not live as disciples of Christ in a historical or theological vacuum. We cannot skip over the centuries to the first century and read the New Testament independent of our own prejudices and heritage. We also do not desire to be arrogant or to be ignorant of the insights and theological developments of others. Baptists have and continue to hear the voices of other Christians on matters of faith and practice. Baptists do believe, however, that the Bible is its own best interpreter. We therefore reject the belief that any church council or ecclesiastical leader can claim to be the sole, authoritative interpreter of the revelation of God.

EXPERIENCE AS THE SOURCE OF RELIGIOUS AUTHORITY

Protestant liberalism asserts that the religious experience of the individual with the divine Spirit constitutes religious authority. Protestant liberalism contends that a divine Spirit pervades the entire creation and is potentially present in all human beings. As a person worships or prays with the right attitude, he encounters the divine Spirit, producing some type of religious experience. Although these events are often described as "indefinable" or "inexplicable," they are considered authoritative for the person who experiences them. Each individual is left to his own devices to interpret the significance and define the nature of the experience for his understanding of the identity of God and the purpose and meaning of life.

Generally speaking, adherents of this position regard the Bible as a great book of religious insight, on the same level as other great religious literature. Proponents of this perspective do not believe the Bible is the written revelation of God.[4]

Another school of thought that views experience as religiously authoritative is neoorthodoxy. It perceives the Bible as the medium through which a person existentially encounters God. In this paradigm, neoorthodoxy does not view the Bible as the objective and authoritative revelation from God. Rather, revelation is the presence of God himself and occurs when the believer meets God. Scripture is not revelation itself but rather bears witness to and is a promise of revelation.[5] The Bible becomes the Word of God when the individual encounters God's presence through its message.[6]

The "revelatory encounter" of neoorthodoxy is what Baptists have classically considered illumination. That is, the moment a person understands religious truth is considered to be the *reception of revelation* (inspiration) by neoorthodoxy, while Baptists (and other evangelicals) view this event as the *reception of understanding* of written revelation (illumination), not revelation.[7] For neoorthodoxy, when the revelation encounter ceases, the Bible is once again simply the words of the men who wrote it. The neoorthodox theologian does not regard the Bible in and of itself as revelatory or authoritative.

Other groups also place authoritative value on religious experience. Enthusiastics, Quakers, and certain mystics claim that the primary religious authority is the Holy Spirit speaking in the heart.[8] This perspective is also found among certain charismatics and Pentecostals. As is the case with any experiential paradigm, the individual is left to his own devices to interpret the nature and meaning of what the Holy Spirit has said to him. Those who adhere to this position regard the authority of the Bible, at best, of secondary importance or, at worst, of no importance at all.

Numerous problems abound with those positions that advocate the authority of religious experience. For example, the foundations of theological liberalism are found in German idealistic philosophy, particularly the philosophy of identity. At its heart, this position rests upon panentheism and therefore confuses the human with the divine. The roots of this theory do not rest on Christian revelation but upon a philosophy influenced by realism, pragmatism, positivism, naturalism, and existentialism.[9]

The neoorthodox position does not fare much better. In neoorthodoxy, there are no revealed truths, only truths of revelation. As such, the truths that one person gleans from a revelatory encounter could be different or even contradictory from the truths discovered by another person. Neoorthodox theologians do not even regard the interpretations of events given by biblical authors to be authoritative. Despite the claims of the adherents of neoorthodoxy, no objective basis for truth claims beyond the existential, revelatory encounters are credibly established. In addition, neoorthodoxy lacks adequate rationale for the Spirit's continued witness through the Bible. Why is the Bible the medium for the divine-human encounter? Why not other religiously oriented literature? Neoorthodoxy does not adequately establish why the Bible is central for this existential encounter.

Few contemporary theologians are prepared to assert that the Holy Spirit alone is the primary authority in religion. There are several reasons for this.

First, this theory in actuality is an experience-based theory, and it suffers from many of the problems inherent in the other experience-based theories.

Second, if this position contends that all inward promptings are from the Spirit, then it must admit that evil and immoral deeds are inspired by the Spirit. If only some of the inward promptings are from the Spirit, then some method of differentiating between what is from the Spirit and what is not must be developed. This would in turn introduce two primary authorities: the Spirit and the method of differentiation.

Finally, what Baptists (and other Protestant Christians) have historically affirmed is that both the written Word and the Holy Spirit are needed.[10]

REASON AS THE SOURCE OF RELIGIOUS AUTHORITY

The philosophers of the Enlightenment, the Deists, and the Unitarians claim that human reason is the sole authority for all truth. This assertion encompasses all matters of truth, including religion and faith. Others argue that, since reason is the means by which the meaning of the Bible is interpreted, reason must be the superior authority.[11]

There are several reasons we as Baptists must reject the belief that reason is an authority superior to the Bible.

First, reason in many ways defies definition. Reason is not a set of axioms that are equally possessed by all human beings. Appeals to reasonableness are typically pleas for comprehensibility, apprehensibility, coherence, and/or consistency. These are not traits that can be known but are rather ways of knowing.

Second, reason is a mode of apprehending truth. The means of knowing should not be confused with what is to be known. In the language of the old theologians, reason has a "ministerial use" (method of apprehension) and not a "magisterial use" (decreeing what is possible and impossible). Reason thus understood may be used "ministerially" for religious truth. The revelation of God is known through the ministerial use of reason, but that does not make reason superior to God's revelation.

Finally, we must remember that reason, like all other human faculties, is affected by human sin. If the human faculty of reason is damaged by sin, then all formulations developed by reason must be judged by another objective authority. Christians have historically contended that all rational claims must be assessed by the objective, written revelation of God.[12]

THE BIBLE AS THE SOURCE OF RELIGIOUS AUTHORITY

As Baptists, we have from our beginning believed that both the Old Testament and New Testament are the inspired and inerrant written revelation of the living God.[13] The Scriptures are the ultimate authority for all matters of faith and practice. We have also believed in the sufficiency of the Scriptures. The Bible reveals what God intended for us to have at each stage of redemptive history. Therefore, it contains all we need for salvation as well as for serving, obeying, and worshipping God. As Baptists, we have also believed that any departure from the teachings of God's Word is evil and sinful. The Bible is our standard for faith and practice in Christianity. It is sufficient in its scope and supreme in its authority.[14]

From our beginning, we have contended that our existence as Baptists is the result of this unwavering commitment to biblical authority. Our Baptist forefathers viewed themselves as the logical outcome to the Reformation principle of *sola scriptura* (the idea that Bible alone is the sole authority for faith and practice). These Baptists made this assertion because they believed that no other Christian denomination was as consistent or as committed in their appeal to and application of the teachings of the Bible for ecclesiastical practice as the Baptists were. Although the majority of Christian denominations theoretically acknowledge that the "Bible alone" is the Word of God, most groups recognize other forms of religious authority, such as religious tradition, reason, or experience. Baptists have historically rejected these other forms of religious authority.

Instead, Baptists have sought to maintain a strict adherence and submission to biblical teaching. This is what distinguishes us and our churches from other Christian denominations. Baptists have historically maintained that our existence arises from our attempt to apply biblical teaching to all realms of life, particularly the church.

The authority of Scripture is a belief that Baptists share generally with other Protestants. As Baptists, however, we contend that we are much more thoroughgoing in this conviction. Other Christians not only affirm biblical authority, but they also regard the decisions of church councils, synods, conferences, or the pronouncements of popes, bishops, and other church leaders as religiously authoritative.

For example, Episcopalians believe in a hermeneutical method commonly called "the three-legged stool." Episcopalians believe that the "three legs of the stool" (Scripture, tradition, and reason) carry equal weight and authority and that this interpretative approach is how Episcopalians determine what is true and good. Episcopal bishop Paul Zahl (who does not endorse this position) succinctly describes this approach as follows: "Ideally, truth, so goes this argument of the 'three-legged stool,' must match with the Bible, the legacy of the church, and the human mind."[15] All three are viewed as equally authoritative for Christian faith and practice.

Baptists categorically reject the view that Scripture, tradition, and reason are of equal weight and authority. This is not to say that Baptists reject a place for tradition and reason in doctrinal development. If the issue under consideration is that we should study church history to guide and direct our biblical interpretations, or if the issue is that human reason assists us to establish coherence and consistency of thought in our understanding of Scripture, Baptists heartily agree. If the issue under consideration, however, is that we must consider church tradition or a certain philosophical system as authoritative as the Bible itself, Baptists emphatically dissent. The Bible stands over and judges church tradition and human reason.

We may highly esteem a certain Christian leader, cherish a particular tradition, or value a specific philosophy. But no leader, tradition, or philosophy can have for Baptists the authority that belongs exclusively to the Lord Jesus Christ as he is revealed to us in his Word. We may respect the judgments and insights of other believers, but we as Baptists believe that we have the right to disagree with the teachings of another if we are convinced from Scripture that such are in error. "Our final authority in matters of faith is the Scriptures, and for us no other authority is final."[16]

Our existence as Baptists is therefore the logical and practical outcome of our belief in the absolute authority of the Bible. As one Baptist theologian has stated, the all-sufficient and authoritative Bible is the "cardinal principle with Baptists."[17] With regard to matters of the Christian faith or practice, the first question we as Baptists must always ask is, "What does the Bible say?" Certain theological ideas, religious institutions, or ministry programs and methods may have a novel attraction about them and may even enjoy initial success among and support of the majority of Christians. But we as Baptists determine the validity of our beliefs, practices, and institutions based upon biblical fidelity.

For example, if a belief or practice is clearly taught in the Bible, then we are bound to accept and adopt that belief or practice. On the other hand, if a belief or practice is contradictory to the meaning of Scripture, we are obligated to reject and oppose the belief or practice. In those instances where there is not a clear or unequivocal teaching on a subject, we as Baptists are free to use our best judgment and follow the convictions of our consciences.

I would argue, however, that even our judgments or convictions should be created and shaped by biblical teaching. "For Baptists, the authority of Scripture is always supreme, and it is this fact more than any other that determines" our belief and practices as well as shapes our judgments and consciences.[18]

We therefore confess as Baptists that the written Word of God stands superior to all other constructs of religious authority found in Christendom, the most common of which are church tradition, religious experience, and human reason. As already noted, the Roman Catholic Church believes that it is the one true church founded by Jesus Christ and that it is gifted with infallibility. The Catholic Church perceives itself as the custodian of the Scriptures and the authoritative interpreter of those Scriptures. For the Roman Catholic, the voice of the church is the voice of Christ. Contrary to this view, Baptists contend that church tradition and pronouncements are under biblical authority. The Word of God constitutes the church, not vice versa. The Bible therefore guides, nourishes, informs, judges, purifies, strengthens, and edifies the church.

The Scriptures are also authoritative over religious experience. The experience of faith in Christ is crucial for the eternal life and spiritual well-being of the individual. The voice of the living God speaking to the individual within the recesses of his soul is life altering. But these faith experiences point us to the reality and need for the objective authority of the Bible. Our experiential encounters with God are correctly understood only when interpreted by the written revelation of God. Religious experience must therefore be guided by and anchored to the Scriptures.

The Bible is also authoritative over culture. Some theologians knowingly or unknowingly derive the content of theology from extrabiblical sources, such as cultural norms or current philosophical trends. As Baptists, we reject such approaches to religious authority. Culture and philosophical insights can assist us in the structure and communication of our beliefs. But the content of our theology must be derived from the Bible alone.

The Bible is authoritative because it is the inspired, inerrant revelation of the living Word of God—Jesus Christ.

The resurrected, ascended Christ is revealed to us through the words of Scripture. The living Word has bound himself to the written Word so that the Bible speaks with the authority of the Lord. The words of Scripture are the words of Christ himself. The Bible is not merely a record of revelation; it is revelation itself. We as Baptists believe and proclaim that the Bible is our authority for all realms of life in general and for matters of Christian faith and practice in particular.

Although written by men, the Bible has God as its ultimate and supreme author. When we read it, we must realize that God is speaking to us from its text. When we refuse to read the Scriptures, we neglect God's Word and refuse to hear his voice. The authority of the Bible is the authority of God himself. The nineteenth-century Baptist theologian, John Leadley Dagg, reminds us of three important truths about the authority of the Bible.

First, the authority of the Bible is supreme. Its promises and precepts are certain and trustworthy. We may rely on the wisdom and instruction of other human beings, but these are fallible and prone to error. We may trust in the authority of governing authorities and societal institutions, but governments can command what is wrong and institutions can lead us astray. God never deceives us or leads us awry. "When the Bible speaks, all else may be silent, and its decisions leave no room for doubt and admit no appeal."

Second, the authority of the Bible is independent. No church, no matter how pure or holy, can infuse the Scriptures with authority. The inspired men who authored the biblical texts did not confer authority upon it; in fact, the biblical authors point to the supernatural, inspiring work of God bringing the Scriptures into being and investing them with his authority. The Bible possesses its authority because it is the Word of God.

Finally, the authority of the Bible is immediate. Its witness is directly from God. We have no mediator but Jesus Christ and no infallible interpreter of the biblical message except the Holy Spirit. We may receive guidance and instruction from human teachers, but only God can illumine our minds and hearts to understand its message.[19]

For Baptists to equate or follow any other standard for the Christian faith is, in a sense, to follow the creature rather than the Creator. To regard our experiences, traditions, or philosophies as equal in authority to the Bible is to regard the thoughts of human beings as equal or superior to the wisdom of God. "Other standards are composed of men's guesses, while in the Bible the great truths of God burn and glow with all the eloquence of heaven. And facing a gainsaying world it becomes us to plant ourselves squarely on God's Word—for we can not do otherwise, God help us—and to point a sin-sick and guilt-blinded race to the open Bible and to the open heaven it reveals."[20]

THE NEW TESTAMENT

Baptists classically affirm the inspiration and authority of both the Old Testament and the New Testament. Doctrines such as the nature and personhood of God, creation, and sin require the authoritative and inspired voice of the Old Testament for theological development. No credible Baptist, past or present, would discount the value and status of the Old Testament as the revelation of God, its vital place in the canon, and its necessity for theological development. The Old

Testament has been and must continue to be included for many of the beliefs that are crucial to the Christian faith.

Our distinctive theological identity as Baptists, however, is derived from the New Testament. As Baptists, we recognize the progressive nature of revelation. Progressive revelation is the belief that later revelation builds upon and expands previous revelation. The New Testament provides revelation on the distinctive traits of Baptists (i.e., our ecclesiology) not revealed in the Old Testament. In this regard, the New Testament supplies and fulfills what is lacking in the Old Testament. Doctrines such as a regenerate church membership, believer's baptism by immersion, and congregational polity can only be developed from the New Testament. Our doctrine of the Baptist church must therefore be constructed from the New Testament.[21]

As was the case with the "Bible alone" emphasis, we believe that Baptists, as New Testament believers, distinguish ourselves from other Christian denominations by constructing our belief and practice on the New Testament. In fact, Baptists have classically believed that applying Old Testament laws to New Testament believers results in deviant and harmful doctrines. B. H. Carroll asserted, "But right here may I state as my firm conviction, that applying Old Testament laws to New Testament times is one of the most fruitful sources of such dark blotches as have marred the record of many professed followers of Christ. This perilous course the Baptists have seen and avoided."[22] Among the deviant and harmful doctrines that we as Baptists consider unbiblical and hurtful to the church are infant baptism, a special priesthood, and state-established churches.

As New Testament believers, Baptists believe that the Old Testament is fulfilled in Christ. Christ is now the lawgiver for

Christians. The New Testament regulates our convictions and conduct, and from it we are to seek direction and instruction for our churches. Baptist leader and statesman B. H. Carroll affirmed that the Old Testament is inspired by God and is profitable for faith and instruction. But he stated that the Old Testament as a "typical, educational, and transitory system" is fulfilled in Christ. According to Carroll, Christ has nailed the Old Testament to the cross, so that "as a standard of law and a way of life" it is "taken out of the way."

New Testament Christians must not look to the Old Testament to find Christian law or Christian institutions because the New Testament has now become the "law" for them. In his classic statement, Carroll strongly asserted this position when he declared, "The New Testament is the law of Christianity. All the New Testament is the law of Christianity. The New Testament is all the law of Christianity. The New Testament will always be all the law of Christianity." This singular emphasis upon the New Testament for faith and practice is a distinguishing conviction between Baptists and other Protestants. "When Baptists say that the New Testament is the only law for Christian institutions they part company, if not theoretically at least practically, with most of the Protestant world, as well as from the Greeks and Romanists."[23]

The New Testament is for Baptists the sole authority and preeminent standard. This conviction serves as the essential distinctive for our theological identity. The ultimate test for any teaching in Christianity is its agreement with the revelation of the New Testament because in it Christ's authority is most clearly revealed. The promises of the Old Testament are fulfilled in the Son of God, "whose majestic person swallowed up all ceremonial law; whose authoritative words, 'but I say unto you,' put new meaning into moral law; and who, as both

Builder and Foundation, established his church in history."[24] The ongoing quest for Baptists is to conform all aspects of faith and practice to the teachings of Jesus Christ as revealed in the New Testament.

The authority of the New Testament is the starting point from which we develop all matters related to church life. Our unyielding commitment to this fundamental principle is what distinguishes our churches from those of other Christian denominations. Our continued vitality and theological distinctiveness is tied to our continued adherence to this tenet. The foundation of our denominational existence and the center of our union as Baptists is influenced by and developed from our singular commitment to the authority of the New Testament.

As one Baptist leader has stated, "Baptists are united in their conviction that the only ultimate standard for Christian faith and practice must be found in conformity to the mind and will of Christ as revealed to us in the New Testament. It is from this fundamental fact that Baptists always start, and with the New Testament in their hands they are ready to deal with every problem of doctrine and conduct that comes."[25]

Our conviction about the primacy of the New Testament impacts and shapes our ecclesiological beliefs and practices. Because this is our core theological conviction, other doctrinal distinctives flow from this basic premise. Following are some of the beliefs that shape the Baptist understanding of the nature and purpose of the church.

First, God is a holy and loving God. As such, he has provided atonement for our sin in the person and work of his Son, Jesus Christ.

Second, as the God-man, Jesus Christ is the only Savior and Lord.

Third, human beings are responsible to God for the life they live on this earth.

Fourth, sin is both an inheritance and a choice.

Fifth, salvation is the regeneration of the person through a divine, gracious act of God.

Sixth, salvation comes through faith in Christ and repentance of sin. As such, the membership of Baptist churches should be comprised only of those persons who have been regenerated and who have professed their faith in believer's baptism by immersion.

Seventh, the redemptive activity of God in the world is manifested through the church. The mission of the church is to proclaim the glory of God as manifested in the gospel of the Son of God.

Eighth, Baptist churches practice congregational church polity and church discipline.

Ninth, the ordinances of baptism and the Lord's Supper commemorate and declare the gospel of Jesus Christ.

Tenth, civil government has a good and providential place in the economy of God. Human governments are, however, limited in their authority.

Eleventh, religious freedom and liberty of conscience are means to ensure the unadulterated proclamation of the gospel, the freedom of individuals to accept or reject the gospel free of coercion, and the integrity of the membership and ministry of the church.

Although several of these doctrinal beliefs are not peculiar to Baptists, the unique combination of these tenets is theologically distinctive to Baptists. We will examine several of these tenets in more detail later.

Baptists formally share with all Protestant Christians the belief that the Bible is the basis for belief and practice. But

Baptists contend that we are much more consistent in this principle, especially with regard to the role the New Testament plays in shaping our theological identity. We attempt to develop all ecclesiological aspects from the New Testament. This conviction is our core distinctive. Although Baptists may disagree about other matters, our commitment to the authoritative role of the New Testament for the development of our understanding of the doctrine of the church has historically been our unifying conviction. As one Baptist leader noted a century ago:

> The all-sufficiency of the Scriptures as a guide in religion is a cardinal principle with Baptists. This eliminates the authority of councils, popes, synods, conferences, bishops, etc. It gives no place to history as a supplement to the teaching of the Bible. It shuts the world up to take the law from the mouth of God. Here we stand, and on this principle we settle all questions. . . . The world wants and sorely needs a centre of unity. That centre is the Word of God. The more it is preached in its fullness, the quicker Christian union will be realized.[26]

IMPLICATIONS

As Baptists, we have always been concerned about "doing church" the right way. More importantly, we have been diligent to establish churches that are built upon the biblical pattern. Any assessment of the health of our Baptist churches must first be in terms of its fidelity to the teachings of the New Testament. With regard to church life, we always start with the question, Do our churches accurately and faithfully reflect what is taught in the New Testament? Our reliance on the New Testament for faith and practice is what safeguards and ensures the proper function of a New Testament church. The Baptist understanding of the church is the attempt of Baptists to reflect their obedience and submission to biblical authority in general and the teachings of the New Testament in particular.

To state it another way, a Baptist church is the visible manifestation of the Baptist commitment to *sola scriptura*.[27] Loyalty to the New Testament is for Baptists the essential expression of a rightly grounded faith and a rightly constituted church.

Our commitment to biblical authority means that we should evaluate all aspects of church life in the light of Scripture. All ministries, programs, ideas, and events must be scrutinized in the light of the revelation of the Bible. This desire to be biblically faithful in all things has always been a part of our theological identity. I have cited the following quotation from R. M. Dudley in another place.[28] It bears repeating because it best illustrates our historical commitment to biblical fidelity in all matters of faith and practice.

> And let me show you how it is that this fundamental principle has led to the separate existence of the Baptists and to the peculiarities that mark their denominational life. . . . Take for example, the question of baptism. Luther said that the primitive baptism was immersion and that the primitive practice should be restored. The Baptists said the same thing and following out of their belief immersed all who came to them even though they had been sprinkled before. Strange to say, for this Luther hated the Baptists hardly less than he hated the Catholics. Calvin said that the word *baptize* means to immerse

and that it is certain that immersion was the practice of the primitive churches, but that in this matter the churches ought to have liberty. Here now are the points of agreement and the points of difference between the Reformers on the one hand and the Baptists on the other. They all agreed that immersion was the practice of the primitive churches. Luther and Calvin thought that they were at liberty to practice another form, the Baptists said that we ought to do what the Master commands; and that we have no liberty to change a positive ordinance which he has ordained. Here the work of separation begins. The issue was not as to what the act of baptism is, but whether we have the right to change it. Before the court of the highest scholarship of the world it has never been an open question as to what the true baptism is. It really is not now, as it was not in the time of Luther and Calvin. The question is about the right to change it; and it is not that Baptists think too much of one form above another. I am frank to say for myself, that if it were a matter left to our choice whether we should immerse or sprinkle, while immersion is a beautiful and significant ordinance and sprinkling is a meaningless ceremony, still I would give up immersion rather than divide Christendom on a mere rite:—I say if it were left to our choice. But it has never been left to our choice: And when others say that they will change the ordinance, the question between them and us is, not what is the true baptism but whether there is any right or authority to change it. Baptists do not yield their position about baptism because it is the surface indication of a great underlying principle. Principles are of use to us because of the guidance they afford us in practical life. What honor or consistency is there in avowing a principle and then denying it in our daily conduct? We see how it is then that the peculiarity of Baptists upon immersion results from their fundamental position. They must be peculiar or they must give up the principle that the Word of God is our supreme and all-sufficient rule.[29]

Dudley also notes that the Baptists reject infant baptism and advocate a memorial view of the Lord's Supper because the New Testament teaches that only professing Christians should be baptized and that grace comes through faith, not the sacraments.

Baptists today must be as committed and faithful to biblical authority as our Baptist ancestors. They modeled for us the practice of assessing all matters of church life in light of the apostolic teaching. If we are to have healthy churches, they must be New Testament churches. In order for our churches to conform to the New Testament, we must know and understand what the New Testament says and be able to apply its teachings consistently and appropriately to our churches.

Church health begins with a commitment to have churches that follow and imbibe the New Testament pattern. If the New Testament is the rule for church life, and if Baptists are right in their ecclesiastical beliefs and practices, then a healthy New Testament church is a Baptist church. To be a Baptist is to be committed to the inspired authority of the New Testament for faith and practice.

Baptists have historically regarded the Bible as the ultimate authority generally for all truth in general and specifically for matters of faith and practice. The authority of the

Bible is a dynamic and vibrant authority, not static or dead. The Scriptures are our source for the historical revelation of God in Christ. As Baptists, we have affirmed that biblical authority regulates and evaluates our Christian experience and is the source for our theological formulations. The objective nature of the revelation of the Bible protects us from complete subjectivism on the one hand and a sterile rationalism on the other.

The Scriptures are the instrument of the Holy Spirit in his regenerative and sanctifying work. The Bible reveals to us the person of the Savior and the power of his saving deeds. The Bible is the final and absolute authority for our Christian faith and practice.

Chapter 2

THE LORDSHIP OF JESUS CHRIST

The lordship of Jesus Christ is the singular, great confession of the Christian faith. When applied to the church, the declaration that "Jesus is Lord" is an absolute affirmation that the church and all that is associated with it belongs to Christ. The lordship of Christ is the belief that the church exists and functions in submission to the person and will of the resurrected Savior. All facets of the life of the church must therefore bear witness to and proclaim the reality of the lordship of Jesus Christ. The proclamation of the gospel, the ministry of church discipline, the acts of mercy to people in crisis, the baptism of believers, the celebration of the Lord's Supper—all in some capacity declare the lordship of Jesus Christ. The church exists to bring all things under his lordship through its presence and its ministry.

As Baptists, we do not claim that the lordship of Christ is our exclusive theological belief. Other Christians certainly

share and affirm this tenet of the faith. Baptists have historically asserted, however, that our distinctive theological identity is shaped by this truth in unique ways.

For example, we believe that Christ's sovereignty cannot
be delegated through human beings or institutions. The person and will of Christ cannot be mediated or manipulated by
any system of human invention. We believe that, whenever
any governing structure attempts to inhibit the lordship of
Christ, the direct and sovereign rule of Christ over the individual and the church is jeopardized. We have historically
rejected any form of ecclesiastical hierarchies. "Any interposi-
tion of ecclesiastical machinery . . . is a manifest impertinence
. . . and always a usurpation and a wrong."[30] No church or religious institution can mediate between Christ and his followers. "No elaborate, impersonal system of rites, ceremonies, and
external forms must be permitted to come between the soul
and the Savior."[31]

A New Testament church strives to appropriate the reality
of this truth. The lordship of Christ must shape the climate,
relationships, witness, and work of our Baptist churches. The
Bible reveals to us the nature and expression of Christ's lordship. We will now investigate what the Scriptures have to say
about the lordship of Christ. Following this, I will then develop
the theological and practical implications of this doctrine for
our understanding of the nature and ministry of a Baptist
church.

BIBLICAL TEACHING ON THE LORDSHIP OF JESUS CHRIST

The Synoptic Gospels contain diverse uses and meanings
of the term *Lord* when applied to Jesus. Many instances of the

use of the term do not designate deity. On some occasions, those who called Jesus "lord" were using the concept as a form of an address to a superior, somewhat in the sense of our modern "sir" (Matt. 8:6). The disciples of Jesus referred to Jesus as "lord" as a designation for rabbi or teacher (Matt. 8:21) or in the sense of "master" (Mark 11:3). After the confession of Simon Peter of Jesus as Lord at Caesarea Philippi, however, the term began to have the sense of messianic king (Matt. 18:21; Luke 12:41; 13:23). Jesus applied the term to himself to indicate his deity (Matt. 24:42; Mark 12:35–37).[32]

The identification of Jesus as Lord in the Book of Acts was a declaration of his deity, suggesting that all that was true of God in the Old Testament was also true of Christ. The lordship of Christ was revealed at Pentecost as Jesus fulfilled his promise to send the Holy Spirit. The sovereignty of Jesus was seen in his ability to keep his promises, even when absent. To send the Spirit was the prerogative of God in the Old Covenant; Jesus was now the sender of the Spirit.

In Peter's Pentecost sermon, he declared that Jesus was the remover of sin (Acts 2:38; see also 7:60; 10:43). The disciples proclaimed that Jesus had the power to act as redeemer and deliverer. These functions—activities considered in the Old Testament to be the sole prerogative of God—were now accredited to Jesus of Nazareth. In the early chapters of Acts, the designation *Lord* connotes the ideas of redeemer (Acts 2:21), savior (Acts 2:21), coming one (Acts 2:20; 10:42), leader (Acts 1:24; 4:29; 5:29; 9:31, 35, 42), sustainer (Acts 7:59–60), eternal one (Acts 10:36; 11:17), judge (Acts 2:20; 10:42), and ruler or authority (Acts 2:34). Because Jesus performed all these functions, the early believers regarded him as the rightful Lord. Jesus was "Lord" in the sense of the exalted, messianic king (Acts 2:36) and the resurrected one (Acts 4:33).

As Lord, Jesus was the one guiding and building the covenant community (Acts 1:24–25; 9:31). The lordship of Jesus Christ was revealed to Stephen to sustain and encourage him during his martyrdom (Acts 7:55, 59). As Lord, Jesus has authority over the Jews and the Gentiles and demonstrates his sovereignty through the inclusion of both groups into the church. Jesus manifests his lordship by judging both the living and the dead (Acts 10:42).[33]

The epistles of the apostle Paul abound with references to Jesus as Lord. Each reference has profound theological implications for the person and work of Christ. For example, Paul declared that the lordship of Christ was revealed through his preexistence and his participation in the creation of the world (1 Cor. 8:6). The genuineness of regeneration and the presence of the Holy Spirit in the life of the believer is revealed through the confession that "Jesus is Lord" (1 Cor. 12:3). The expression "Our Lord, come!" (1 Cor. 16:22) may be a reference to the second coming of Christ, a reference to his presence in the worship of the congregation, or both.

As Lord, Jesus is designated as "the powerful Son of God by the resurrection from the dead according to the Spirit of holiness" (Rom. 1:4). The earliest confession of redeemed believers was "Jesus is Lord," which accompanied the inner conviction that God raised Christ from the dead (Rom. 10:9). The universal confession of all creation at the Last Judgment and in the final state will also be "Jesus Christ is Lord" (Phil. 2:11)

Although Christ's lordship is not as prominent a theme in the general epistles as in the other New Testament writings, they also mention the lordship of Christ. The apostle Peter noted that knowledge (i.e., personal experience) of Christ's lordship safeguards against unfruitful service and the impurity of the world (2 Pet. 1:8; 2:20) as well as facilitates growth in grace (2 Pet. 3:18). Peter also connected the blessings of God the Father to Christ's lordship, entrance into the kingdom of God in this life and the life to come, and the Second Coming (1 Pet. 1:3; 2 Pet. 1:11, 14, 16). Jude mentioned the lordship of Christ as a source of strength for Christians living in the midst of false teachings, persecutions, and ungodly and immoral practices (Jude 4, 17, 21, 25). The author of Hebrews stated that our great salvation was first declared by the Lord (Heb. 2:3), who is the resurrected Lord and the Great Shepherd of the sheep (Heb. 13:20).

The Johannine writings have numerous references to the concept of Jesus as Lord. In his Gospel, the apostle John noted several occasions when Jesus was called "Lord": Peter (John 6:68; 13:6, 9; 13:37); the man blind from birth (John 9:38); Mary and Martha (John 11:3, 21, 27, 32, 39); John (John 13:25); Thomas (John 14:5); Philip (John 14:8); and Judas (John 14:22). These uses seem to be the equivalent of Messiah or Son of God. The designations of Jesus as Lord in the post-resurrection chapters signify his deity (John 20–21). The direct confessions of Jesus as Lord by Thomas (John 20:28) and Peter (John 21:15–17) also refer to his deity. Although the most common use of the term *Lord* in the Book of Revelation is to God the Father, Jesus is also called "Lord Jesus" (Rev. 22:20–21), "Lord of lords and King of kings" (Rev. 17:14), and "King of kings and Lord of lords" (Rev. 19:16).

The New Testament teaching of the lordship of Jesus Christ emphasizes both his lordship over creation and his lordship over his church. His lordship over the created order includes all creatures, unseen powers, human governments, and the entire universe. According to the apostle Paul, Christ will eventually hand his kingdom over to God the Father when the end comes (1 Cor. 15:24), at which time all earthly rule, authority, and power will be abolished. Although the reality of his rule is certain, unbelievers live oblivious to his governance and in rebellion against it. The presence and power of sin must now be biblically and theologically interpreted in light of Christ's sovereignty.[34]

Many of the biblical and postbiblical instances of the phrase "Jesus is Lord" are designations of his full deity, equal in divinity to God the Father. The earliest confession of the church ("Jesus is Lord") distinguished those who believed in Jesus from those who did not. This confession came to identify those who were truly the disciples of Jesus Christ. The term *lord* had powerful linguistic and theological connotations; most notably the term was used to translate the Tetragrammaton (the four Hebrew characters used to represent the sacred name of God in Hebrew). The translation of the Hebrew word could be "Yahweh." It was regarded as improper to pronounce the name of God; an alternative word (*adonai*) was used in Hebrew.

In the Septuagint (the Greek translation of the Old Testament), the word *kurios* (lord) was used to translate the Tetragrammaton. *Kurios* eventually came to be reserved for God. The first-century Jews recognized that use of the term *kurios* for any person other than God was idolatrous and that the word should only be used in referring to God.[35]

TWO ASPECTS OF CHRIST'S SOVEREIGNTY

The lordship of Christ is first of all an objective truth. Christ rules sovereignly over all things. His rule is absolute. We commonly hear some Christians say something like, "We need to make Jesus Lord." We do not make him Lord; he is Lord by virtue of his person. There is only one Lord, God the Son, through whom, in whom, and to whom are all things (Col. 1:15–20). All things were made by him and will be summed up in him. Through his incarnation, the Lord became one with humanity in order to be its Savior. By virtue of his atonement, he reigns over mankind as Redeemer and Judge (cf. Acts 17:31).

Christ has authority and achieved authority by his saving death and victorious resurrection. The ascended Christ now sits at the right hand of the Father, continually making intercession for those who belong to him. The result of his completed work of atonement is a fuller assertion of his lordship over all things.[36] Whether an individual personally experiences Christ's lordship in no way affects the objectivity of his rule. Jesus Christ is Lord over all creation and declares his lordship in the Great Commission: "All authority has been given to Me in heaven and on earth" (Matt. 28:18).[37]

The lordship of Christ is secondarily a subjective truth. The lordship of Christ is crucially important for our understanding of salvation. The confession of the Christian faith from its inception has been "Jesus is Lord." The Bible indicates that this profession is possible only by the presence and work of the Holy Spirit in the life of a believer (1 Cor. 12:3). The subjective element is experienced in the personal appropriation of Christ's rule in the hearts and lives of individual believers in their salvation experience. The Christian faith is essentially the vital union between God and man through Jesus Christ. The lordship of Christ asserts that no person or human institution can mediate or interfere with the relationship between the King and his subjects. Religious systems, ceremonies, or external practices must not be permitted to come between the believer and the Master.

THEOLOGICAL MEANING OF THE LORDSHIP OF CHRIST

DEITY

The confession "Jesus is Lord" is a declaration of his full deity. As already noted, the term *lord* that was reverently and uniquely applied to the God of the Abrahamic covenant would also be ascribed to Jesus of Nazareth. The lordship of Christ is most clearly revealed in the light of his resurrection although indicators of his lordship were revealed before his crucifixion. Jesus Christ is the living Lord, who exerts and manifests his sovereign rule from the exalted status at the right hand of the Father.

The reality of the lordship of Christ is realized and appropriated through the presence of the Holy Spirit. The designation "Lord" must be exclusively reserved for Jesus Christ alone. To declare that Jesus is Lord is to confess that he alone is the sole Sovereign. In a pluralistic context that affirms the validity of countless world religions, heretical cults, and atheistic or humanistic beliefs, the declaration of the lordship of Christ is counter-cultural and singularly distinctive.[38]

The lordship of Christ is a revelation of the sovereignty of God in general and of the Son of God in particular. The incarnation of God in Christ is "the greatest of all conceivable expressions" of divine sovereignty. The incarnation, ministry, death, resurrection, and ascension of Jesus Christ reveal that the sovereign Lord has taken the initiative in salvation and is the revelation of full deity. The sovereign Lord has achieved and is working to reconcile God with man.

One of the greatest demonstrations of divinity is the creation of life. Because Jesus is Lord, he has the power to give life. As previously noted, numerous passages in the New Testament connect Christ's lordship to the resuscitation of Lazarus from the dead, his own resurrection from the dead, the regeneration of believers with spiritual life, and the resurrection of believers from the dead. As a demonstration of Christ's divine authority, the same power that subjects all things under his sovereign rule also imparts resurrected life to those who are believers, conforming us as his subjects "into the likeness of His glorious body" (Phil. 3:21). The giving of life in creation, in human life, in the new birth, and in the resurrection demonstrates that the Lord has conquered and subjected our greatest enemy: death (physical, spiritual, and eternal) under his divine rule.[39]

DOMINION

The lordship of Jesus also indicates his complete dominion. To confess that Jesus is Lord is to confess that Jesus is Ruler. Christ is Lord over his creation and his church. The proclamation of the gospel in the early church was to call upon sinners to submit themselves to the lordship of Christ. The early Christians believed that they lived under the dominion of the Lord Jesus. Recent attempts in evangelicalism to divorce the lordship of Christ from the preaching of the gospel and the Christian life are a distortion of biblical revelation. The separation of the saviorhood of Jesus from the lordship of Jesus is contrary to the overall witness of the New Testament.[40]

As Baptists, we believe that the church exists under a Christocracy. Christ rules absolutely and immediately over those who belong to him. E. Y. Mullins referred to this rule of Christ as "an absolute monarchy," the most absolute the world has ever known. The monarch is in heaven, and he relates to his subjects through his divinely revealed word and the presence of the Holy Spirit. Christ's subjects have direct fellowship and interaction with him. Jesus communes with his followers directly through a personal relationship with him as well as corporately through his interaction and rule over his church.[41]

The whole of creation comes under the complete lordship of Jesus. He is the sovereign firstborn over all creation, since it was created through him and is sustained by him (Col. 1:15–16; Heb. 1:3). The structure of Colossians 1:15–20 suggests that Jesus has the same relationship over the created order that he has over his new creation, the church. Because he sustains all things by his powerful word (Heb. 1:3), Jesus providentially guides and governs all aspects of creation.[42] The purpose of God is to bring all things (creation and church) to their fulfillment in the Lord (Eph. 1:10).[43]

DIRECTION

The lordship of Jesus includes his direct guidance of his disciples. This direction occurs through their obedient surrender and the increasing conformity of their lives to his will. Jesus called for his disciples to hear and obey all his teachings (Matt. 7:24–27; 28:20) and to follow him in discipleship and self-renunciation (Mark 8:34). Their loyalty to him was to transcend their love for earthly possessions (Luke 18:22) and family allegiances (Luke 9:59–62; 14:16). Because of the nature of his lordship and the extent of his rule, the lordship of Jesus demands complete and unequivocal surrender. For the Christian, to declare "Jesus is Lord" is to commit to live in obedience to his teachings and to submit to his direction of their lives by the Holy Spirit.[44]

IMPLICATIONS FOR THE CHURCH

The doctrine of the lordship of Christ has been present in Baptist life since our beginning. Following our commitment to the authority of the New Testament, the lordship of Christ is one of our Baptist distinctives. Several examples from Baptist history bear witness to this truth. The classic statement by John Smyth in 1610 gives evidence of the early presence of this belief among Baptists: "Christ only is king and lawgiver of the church and conscience." Thomas Armitage stated in 1890: "The living and underlying principles of Baptist Churches relate to the sovereign and absolute headship of Christ in his Churches."[45] Another Baptist leader noted that "Baptists have always held this doctrine of Christ's supreme headship as one of their most spiritual possessions. It lies at the basis of their polity and furnishes the keynote of their history."[46]

As Baptists, we have always claimed as part of our theological heritage the sovereignty of Christ. We have also exemplified a dogged determination to ensure a full and consistent recognition of his personal and direct authority over the souls of men.[47]

Christ's sovereignty has direct bearing upon the Baptist understanding of the church. In every Baptist congregation, each member is responsible and accountable to Christ as Lord. This doctrine has both individual and corporate implications. Individual believers who are not rightly related to a local congregation are not fully submitted to Christ's lordship. In addition, each member is responsible to participate in the ministry of the local church. A person's participation in the ministry of a local church is in part a declaration by him of his surrender to Christ's lordship.

The corporate aspect of Christ's lordship is revealed as the congregation collectively submits itself to his direction. The church is not a collection of "ministries"; rather, the members of the congregation function together corporately and singularly in the ministry of the lord of the church. The lordship of Christ is thus a declaration of his ownership and rulership over the church. He purchased the church with his blood. He owns the church; the members of the congregation are simply the stewards of his possession.

The doctrine of the lordship of Christ is a declaration that the risen Lord is presently at work in his church. All facets of the members of a church live under his lordship (Rom. 14:8). The baptism of the Holy Spirit is the act of the risen Lord through which he creates, empowers, and extends his church. Through the presence and ministry of the Spirit, the lordship of Jesus is exercised in such a way that even the work of the Spirit is considered to be the work of the risen Lord. The Lord exercises his lordship in part by bestowing church leaders for the equipping of the saints and the perfecting of his body (Eph. 4:11–13). The diversity and types of giftings are the declaration of the victory of the Lord over the grave and a demonstration of his sovereignty over the church (1 Cor. 12:4–11).

The lordship of Christ underscores his leadership and direction of his people. Through the witness of the Word and the Spirit, Jesus provides direct guidance for the church as it functions in its mission. The written revelation of God is the standard through which the Lord speaks to his church. The Scriptures express the authority and will of Christ, and they evaluate and define any and all personal experiences that individual believers may have with the resurrected Lord. The Bible therefore teaches us the nature of his lordship and how that lordship is manifested and experienced individually and corporately. Jesus Christ will not exercise his lordship contrary to the teachings of Scripture.

In addition, each local congregation must always define its purpose and ministry in light of and in submission to the King of kings. Since the lordship of Christ provides the reason for the existence of the church, all a church is and does should ultimately point to the Lord of the church. Drawing upon the body-head imagery developed by Paul, the church derives its empowerment from the Head of the church, who sustains his body and directs its course in its fulfillment of the Lord's divine plan (Eph. 1:22–23; Col. 1:18; 2:10). In this sense, the risen Lord continues and extends the ministry he began in his incarnation while on earth.

Through the Spirit, the risen Lord facilitates prayer, praise, thanksgiving, and intercession as regular activities in the life of the church. The church finds occasion for worship and celebration in the truth and reality of Christ's lordship (Rom. 5:11; Phil. 3:1; 4:4). As one expression of his lordship, the resurrected Christ has promised to be with his church in its ministry and witness to the nations throughout the ages (Matt. 28:19–20). From his place of authority at the right hand of the Father, the lordship of Christ ensures the unceasing flow of the love of God to believers. His lordship also guarantees his ability to keep believers eternally secure in his love and power (Rom. 8:34–39).

The lordship of Christ ensures the ultimate success of his church in its ministry and proclamation in history. The church is not ultimately bound in allegiance to human governance or authority; rather, the church finds freedom for service in submission and allegiance to the risen Lord. Because Christ is Lord of the church, the body of believers is to focus on faithfulness and obedience, resting in the fact that ultimate success comes from the one who gives the increase (1 Cor. 3:6).

Even the most formidable and last enemy of the church (death) has already been conquered, and its demise is rendered certain by the victorious Lord (1 Cor. 15:25–26). Victory in spiritual warfare is assured because of the conquest of the Lord over sin and the demonic horde. The church of Jesus Christ therefore finds freedom and purpose in the reality of Christ's lordship.

Chapter 3

A REGENERATE CHURCH MEMBERSHIP

Discussions regarding Baptist identity and belief naturally lead to discussion of the Baptist idea of the church. The rise of Baptists in the history of Christianity can be understood in part as the desire of a group of earnest believers to have a church that exists and functions in complete submission to the authority of the New Testament. The doctrine of a regenerate church membership is one logical and natural conclusion of the Baptist commitment to biblical authority. In fact, an emphasis upon a regenerate church membership has historically been so dominant in Baptist life that some Baptist leaders have contended that this theological tenet is the core distinctive for Baptists.

For example, J. B. Jeter noted that "a spiritual, or regenerate, church membership . . . lies at the foundation of all Baptist peculiarities."[48] I have noted elsewhere, however, that the idea of a regenerate church membership as the core theological distinctive of Baptists is essentially the outworking of a thorough commitment to biblical authority.[49]

Baptists have historically believed that a church submitted to the authority of the New Testament for faith and practice is a healthy church. Baptists have further believed that the New Testament teaches that churches are ideally to be composed only of regenerate persons. For Baptists, church health has been and must continue to be shaped by the conversion of its members. Christ has determined that only those who have experienced the new birth can be members of his church. Churches that are submitted to the authority and teachings of the New Testament should admit into their memberships only those who can give testimony and evidence that they have been born again. Baptists have therefore considered a regenerate church membership as one necessary component for a healthy church and an essential prerequisite for membership in a Baptist church.

BIBLICAL TEACHING ON A REGENERATE CHURCH MEMBERSHIP

In order to understand our Baptist commitment to the ideal of a regenerate church membership, we should investigate what the Bible has to say about the matter. Intimations to our concept of a regenerate membership can be found in the Old Testament.

The prophet Jeremiah declared that a day was coming when the sovereign Lord would make a new covenant with the houses of Israel and Judah. In that day, God would place his law in the hearts of his people, causing them to love and obey him as never before (Jer. 31:31–33; 32:39–40).

The prophet Ezekiel stated that the Spirit of God would purify his people from their defilement and would give them a new heart, creating for himself a new people (Ezek. 11:19–20). God further announced through his prophet: "I will also sprinkle clean water on you, and you will be clean. I will cleanse you from all your impurities and all your idols. I will give you a new heart and put a new spirit within you; I will remove your heart of stone and give you a heart of flesh. I will place My Spirit within you and cause you to follow My statutes and carefully observe My ordinances" (Ezek. 36:25–27). Regeneration in the Old Testament was thus the work of God renewing and creating a people for himself.

The New Testament contains the fullest and clearest teaching on the concept of regeneration. The concept of the new birth is a significant theme in the writings of the apostle John. In his Gospel, the apostle recounted the discourse of Jesus with Nicodemus in which the Lord described the regenerating activity of God as the birth "from above" or "born again" (John 3:3, 7) and as a birth "of water and the Spirit" (John 3:5, 8). In the prologue to his Gospel, John also mentioned being born "of God" (John 1:13). The aorist or perfect tense of the verb *gennaō* is used in the Book of John to denote the once-for-all divine work of God. In regeneration (or new birth), God infuses into sinners spiritual life by which they are enabled to participate in spiritual activities and to receive the privileges and blessings that God bestows on his children.

Although the term *regeneration* is not found in his epistles, John does develop the concept. For example, the apostle noted that "everyone who has been born of God does not sin, because His seed remains in him; he is not able to sin, because he has been born of God" (1 John 3:9). "Dear friends, let us love one another, because love is from God, and everyone who loves has been born of God and knows God" (1 John 4:7). "We know that everyone who has been born of God does not sin, but the One who is born of God keeps him, and the evil one does not touch him" (1 John 5:18). The present tense of the verb suggests a habitual life of sin rather than perfect sinlessness.

Those who are regenerate love Christians (1 John 4:7) and experience victory over the world (1 John 5:4). In spite of what they might claim, those who live otherwise are unregenerate and are children of the devil (1 John 3:6–10). For John, the regenerate life is a "*sine qua non* for being one of the community of Christians."[50]

The concept of regeneration is also found in other New Testament writings. The apostle Paul spoke of being "baptized into His death" (Rom. 6:3). He also presented the idea of new life as a co-resurrection with Christ (Eph. 2:5; Col. 2:13) and as a work of recreation (or new creation) in Christ (2 Cor. 5:17; Eph. 2:10; Gal. 6:15). Titus 3:5 states that God "saved us—not by works of righteousness that we had done, but according to His mercy, through the washing of regeneration and renewal by the Holy Spirit." The apostle Peter described the concept of regeneration as "a new birth" (1 Pet. 1:3) and as being "born again" (1 Pet. 1:23). James also declared that the new birth comes by means of the "message of truth" (James 1:18).

The New Testament clearly teaches that to be in the Christian community, a person must have been "born of God." But we should not conclude that the New Testament teaches that the churches are sinless. Nothing could be further from the truth. John warned his readers, "If we say, 'We have no sin,' we are deceiving ourselves, and the truth is not in us" (1 John 1:8). The epistle of 1 Corinthians clearly reveals the imperfect condition of those whom Paul describes as saints in the church at Corinth. Paul's statement of Christ's giving of himself for the church so that he might "present the church to Himself in splendor, without spot or wrinkle or any such thing, but holy and blameless" (Eph. 5:27) points to the yet unrealized perfection of the community of believers.

We thus have a tension in the New Testament between the ideal and the actual holiness of the members of the churches of Christ. The dialectic between regeneracy and degeneracy precipitated the need and practice for church discipline in the New Testament. We will discuss this doctrine in more detail in the next chapter. But I do want to note at this time that the doctrines of a regenerate church membership and church discipline are vitally linked. Church discipline can stimulate holiness and edification (both personal and corporate) as well as rebuking, censuring, and disfellowshipping those who refuse to repent of their sin and submit themselves to the authority of Christ (evidences of the absence of the regenerating work of God).

The practice of church discipline by the early church was one way to work for the ideal of a regenerate church membership. This discipline is a biblical process designed to remove unregenerate persons who may have been admitted into the fellowship of the regenerate.

A REGENERATE CHURCH MEMBERSHIP IN BAPTIST THOUGHT

The concept of a regenerate church membership has been a crucial doctrine for Baptists since our beginning. The concept of the new birth and its implications for church membership was a prominent theme among the Anabaptists. Conrad

Grebel, a leader among the Swiss Brethren, taught that converts should be received into the membership of New Testament churches only after giving evidence of having died to self and having been raised with Christ.[51]

The first writing of Menno Simons following his renunciation of Roman Catholicism was entitled *The Spiritual Resurrection*.[52] In his treatise entitled *The New Birth*, Menno contended that those who are truly regenerate should become active and faithful members of the church, "Companions of the body of Christ."[53] The concept of regeneration was a prominent theme in all his writings. Dietrich Philips, a Dutch Anabaptist, argued for the necessity of the new birth for entrance into the membership of the church of God.[54]

The idea of a regenerate church membership was also an important theme in early Baptist writings. Of the One Hundred Articles set forth by the English Baptist congregation of John Smyth in Amsterdam, nineteen specifically mention or address regeneration, the regenerates, or the new creation.[55] The Somerset Particular Baptist Confession states that "in admitting members into the church of Christ, it is the duty of the church, and ministers whom it concerns, in faithfulness to God, that they be careful they receive none but such as do make forth evident demonstration of the new birth, and the work of faith with power."[56]

The Second London Confession, which became by the addition of two articles the Philadelphia Confession of Faith, states that "all persons throughout the world, professing the faith of the gospel, and obedience unto God by Christ, according unto it; not destroying their own profession by any errors everting the foundation, or unholiness of conversation, are and may be called visible saints; and of such ought all particular congregations to be constituted."[57] The New Hampshire

Confession of Faith contains an article on regeneration although it doesn't make explicit the connection between regeneration and church membership.[58]

The Charleston Baptist Church Discipline gives detailed procedures for the admission of members upon evidence of regeneration. The Charleston Discipline states, "Except a man be born again, he has no right to enter into the kingdom of God nor into a gospel church," and "none are fit materials for a Gospel-Church without having first experienced an entire change of nature."[59] To open the door of membership "so wide as to suffer unbelievers, unconverted and graceless persons to crowd into it without control" is "to make the Church of Christ a harlot."[60] Although the Baptist Faith and Message (2000; also 1925 and 1963) underscores the importance and necessity of regeneration, this confession of faith makes no direct connection between regeneration and church membership.

A sampling of Baptist theologians also reveals the necessity of regeneration for church membership. After listing various descriptions for the early church found in the New Testament, John Leadley Dagg concluded that "no doubt can exist that these churches were . . . composed of persons truly converted to God."[61] A. H. Strong connected regeneration with church membership in his definition of the universal church ("The church of Christ . . . is the whole company of regenerate persons in all times and ages, in heaven and on earth") and the visible church ("the individual church may be defined as that smaller company of regenerate persons, who, in any given community, unite themselves voluntarily together, in accordance with Christ's laws, for the purpose of securing the complete establishment of his kingdom in themselves and in the world").[62]

W. T. Conner likewise underscored the importance of regeneration for church membership:

> That the church should be composed of the regenerate only, the New Testament makes clear. . . . Moreover, the nature and mission of the church carries with it the view that only regenerate people should belong to the church. . . . Moreover, if regeneration is an absolute necessity to Christian character and regeneration depends on voluntary acceptance of the gospel, then for a child to be reared in the church . . . without regeneration is a perilous thing. . . . The question as to who should be baptized will have an important bearing on the question of a regenerate church membership.[63]

James Leo Garrett calls upon Southern Baptists to reclaim their heritage of a regenerate church membership.[64] Millard J. Erickson states that the church "is to be a fellowship of regenerate believers who display the spiritual qualities of their Lord."[65] Gordon Lewis and Bruce Demarest stipulate that a church is to be composed only of those who have been regenerated.[66] Wayne Grudem defines the church as the community of all *true* believers for all time; that is, only those who are truly "born again" should be included into the membership of a local church.[67]

IMPORTANCE OF A REGENERATE CHURCH MEMBERSHIP

One crucial element that distinguishes a New Testament church is that only regenerate persons are admitted into its membership. If the church is truly a spiritual body, then only those who are truly spiritual should be allowed entrance into its fellowship. Those who are admitted into membership should give evidence that they have "passed from death to life" (John 5:24). These persons should also readily and willingly confess their allegiance to Jesus Christ as Lord and Savior. Those churches that strive to conform to the teaching of the New Testament will receive none but those who profess their faith in believer's baptism. Those persons who do not live in submission to Christ's lordship and who do not conform their lives to the teachings of the Bible should be excluded from membership.

We Baptists have never pretended that we can play the role of God and know the thoughts or the heart of a person. But we do believe that judgments can be made about who should and should not belong to our churches. We do understand the importance of a person's confession of faith and that only those who make this profession through believer's baptism should be admitted into the membership of our churches. Even in this we are not perfect. We have made and will continue to make errors in judgment. Any Baptist church will have some people who are unregenerate. But we do attempt to do all that is biblically right and appropriate to restrict our membership to Christians, to those who are truly regenerate and have openly professed their faith in Jesus Christ as Lord and Savior.

The church is to be a holy, spiritual body of people. Only persons who have been regenerated by the Holy Spirit should be admitted into the membership of a local church. The teaching and pattern of the New Testament overwhelmingly support this contention. Any church that intentionally allows, through doctrine or practice, unregenerate persons into membership violates the teachings of Scripture and perverts the very nature of the gospel itself. A church is the body of Christ and is to be composed of believers who belong to that body as living members (1 Cor. 12:12–27). Each member of the body must be alive; that is, he or she must be regenerated. Each person must by the power of the Holy Spirit be spiritually enabled to function and discharge the spiritual functions as a member of the church.

The living Christ dwells in his church. He speaks, walks, and works in and through it (1 Cor. 3:16; 2 Cor. 6:16). If the unregenerate join the fellowship of the redeemed, "then Christ's body has become afflicted with dead members, and the very nature of that church is perverted and its work hindered."[68]

The doctrine of a regenerate church membership, coupled with believer's baptism, distinguishes us from other Christian denominations. We as Baptists have historically rejected the practice of infant baptism as unbiblical and as a perversion of the gospel. Only those persons capable of professing Christ for themselves should be admitted into the membership of a church. Infant baptism is contrary to and in conflict with belief in a regenerate membership. No one is eligible for church membership who has not first been brought into a personal, spiritual relationship with Christ through the new birth.

The biblical sequence of events is that regeneration occurs first, followed by church membership. Infant baptism reverses this order. Those who receive infant baptism are in some way considered to be part of the covenant community, regardless of whether they have been truly born again. The new birth is a personal experience that comes only to those who are capable of making a faith commitment to Christ. We believe that infants are incapable of making such a commitment.

Our understanding of the nature of the church is thus intertwined with our understanding of regeneration. Any church that formally or informally diminishes or eliminates regeneration as a necessary condition for church membership denies biblical truth and perverts the spiritual essence of the church.

Our conviction for a regenerate church membership is not an arrogant claim that all those who are members of Baptist churches are truly converted. My contention is that, when we are faithful to this conviction, we will intentionally attempt to exclude unregenerate persons from church membership. Baptists deliberately strive for the ideal of a truly converted, regenerated church membership. "Baptists, by admitting only the regenerate into their membership, are the only people who even in theory stand for the pure spirituality of the churches."[69]

Infant baptism either presupposes that infants are truly regenerated and are therefore members, or that the infants who are baptized are not truly regenerated but are regarded as members. In either scenario, churches that baptize infants have a practice that intentionally conveys church membership upon unregenerate persons. Further, this practice conveys the false belief that unregenerate infants who have been baptized are in right standing with God.

The emphasis on this doctrine underscores the spiritual nature of the church. The church is a spiritual body, created, filled, nourished, and guided by the Holy Spirit. Only those who have the life of the Spirit (i.e., those who are regenerated) can and should comprise the membership of the church. A regenerated church membership is made up of persons who have surrendered themselves to Christ and who share a common faith and communion with God and with others.

According to the New Testament, persons regenerated by the Spirit of God are also adopted into the family of God. The church is thus a family of the regenerate, a group of people who are united in a society jointly submitted to the lordship of Christ and are indwelt by the Holy Spirit. Unregenerate persons cannot and do not share in these blessed realities. Therefore, they neither physically nor spiritually share in the church's membership.[70]

Regeneration is a prerequisite for church membership. The church does not and cannot impart spiritual life or grace through the sacraments. Regeneration occurs only by the gracious, saving act of God. Although some Christian groups believe the church is the place where salvation is dispensed, Baptists believe that the church "is not a savior, but the home of the saved."[71]

The doctrine of a regenerate church membership is a necessary safeguard to protect the integrity and vitality of the church's message and mission. An unregenerate membership is a worldly and carnal membership. At best, such a church will be irrelevant or ineffective in its beliefs and practices. At worst, it will abandon orthodox belief and practice altogether. The ability of a spiritual community to function effectively in its spiritual mission therefore presupposes a spiritually regenerated community of believers. The work, witness, and worship of the church mandate the spiritual regeneration of the members of the fellowship.

No unregenerate person could ever relate spiritually to believers, practice the spiritual disciplines, or participate in the spiritual ministry. Any belief or practice that diminishes this doctrine jeopardizes the ability of a church to fulfill its biblical mandate. To neglect or ignore this theological tenet is to allow the world to infiltrate and influence the church, diminishing its effectiveness in its kingdom mission.[72] Regeneration is the means by which the privileges and responsibilities of church life are attained. The proper execution of the church in its mission requires that regenerate people perform its ministries.

CHALLENGES TO A REGENERATE CHURCH MEMBERSHIP

I have noticed in recent years a marked decline in the emphasis on a regenerate church membership in Baptist life. Few people in Baptist life seem overly concerned about this growing trend. Southern Baptists in particular seem to be drifting further away from this ideal. Baptist pulpits are strangely silent on the subject. Baptist churches seem to relax more and more their standards for admission into church membership. I am afraid that, if current trends continue, Baptists will lose one of their distinctive theological tenets.

In 1961, James Leo Garrett identified and addressed many of the same concerns that still confront Baptists today. At that time, he noted that there were varying degrees of drifting away from a belief in a regenerate church membership and varying degrees of awareness of the problem. I believe that the problems and oversights that existed then are even greater today. We have drifted further away from our conviction and implementation of this doctrine over the years, and fewer Baptists seem to be aware or concerned about this departure from this core tenet of our Baptist identity. Without attempting to distinguish causes from symptoms, Garrett offered some critical insights into this dilemma that I believe are still relevant and demand our attention and action.

First, new converts seeking membership in our Baptist churches are no longer required to give public confessions of their own faith or to provide public testimony of their conversion. Pastors, evangelists, or other church leaders instead relate the testimony or make the confession for the person. In so doing, Baptists have informally adopted a proxy method for the public confession of faith! When a person does speak, any questions put to the applicant are framed in such a way that the answers are implied in the question or are readily self-evident. Garrett notes that the tendency of Baptist churches to vote on candidates for membership after such superficial processes make the vote a meaningless exercise.[73]

Second, some Southern Baptist churches lack any serious doctrinal or ethical standards for membership. This phenomenon has cheapened the meaning of church membership. A "believe what you will" and "do what you please" attitude permeates many Baptist churches. Baptist congregations should establish doctrinal, ethical, and fellowship standards and should clearly state such standards to any person seeking membership in their churches. As Garrett notes, "If civic clubs, fraternal orders, and voluntarist societies of various types have stricter standards for membership than Southern Baptist churches, this brings no credit to the latter and no honor to our Lord Jesus Christ."[74]

Third, Southern Baptist life is immersed in a culture that measures ministerial and ecclesiastical success numerically. Pastors and other church leaders are overwhelmed with the pressure to produce results. Statistical growth has replaced biblical fidelity as the standard for ministerial excellence. This climate encourages churches to lower their membership requirements. The emphasis on a regenerate church membership may diminish in order to "grow the church" or to "have a big church." Church growth is typically defined in terms of multiplication to the exclusion of maturation.

Fourth, leading questions or semicoercive methods may account for spurious professions of faith. Questionable methods produce questionable results. Manipulative tactics often target children, which accounts for the ever-decreasing age of conversion in many Southern Baptist churches.

Fifth, the widespread method of voting on new applicants practiced in many Baptist churches can also be a contributing factor to the lack of emphasis on a regenerate church membership. The common practice is to vote on new members immediately after the applicant has presented himself for membership. Some churches justify this practice on the ground that the pastor or other church representative has already conferred and examined the candidates before they present themselves. Although this may in theory be the case, such practices tend to be the exception rather than the rule. Membership interviews conducted before congregational voting are rare. Those who do interview applicants before the vote still must contend with those who present themselves publicly for membership without any interview.

Baptists would do well to vote on applicants for membership only after satisfactory interviews and dialogues have occurred in which the requirements and expectations of membership in a Baptist church are clearly explained to the candidates. These methods would alleviate the pressure to make immediate and undiscerning decisions that the public formats and time constraints often create.[75]

Southern Baptists (and all Baptists for that matter) would do well to hearken to the concerns identified by Garrett. Failure to heed these warnings will result in irreparable harm to our churches. The loss of the conviction of a regenerate church membership would be the abandonment of one of our crucial theological distinctives. We would in essence forsake one of our core tenets that has classically and theologically defined us as Baptists in the free church tradition. We would erase the line of demarcation between the church and the world.

Our churches would become more worldly and carnal and less holy and Christlike. We would witness an increase in the number of inactive, indifferent, uncommitted, and undedicated members in our churches. In our effort to have larger churches with greater numbers of members, we would contribute to the demise of effective evangelism and witness a decrease in the number of new converts. We would also lose our prophetic voice to speak with biblical convictions on the great moral and social issues of our day.[76]

Baptists do not advance the cause of Christ by compromising our convictions on this matter. The drift toward irrelevancy can be reversed by reclaiming and applying this biblical tenet for church life. The doctrine of a regenerate church membership will motivate us to seek the initiative and power of God to conform our churches to the biblical pattern.

CONCLUSION

The doctrine of a regenerate church for Baptists is the belief that local congregations are to be composed only of those who have and continue to give evidence of the new birth that comes from the Holy Spirit. The membership of visible, local churches is to consist only of persons who have received spiritual life and who live in fellowship with Christ and with Christian brothers and sisters. Although unregenerate people may be included in various meetings and ministries of a local church, the membership of the congregation is to be regenerate. This doctrine impacts both the admission of members to a congregation and the proper maintenance of the church membership.

A regenerate church membership points to the personal nature of salvation. Regeneration implies repentance of sin, a changed nature, a new heart, and a surrendered will. A regenerate church membership also points to the voluntary surrender of the individual and the corporate body to the lordship of Jesus Christ. The outward act of believer's baptism signifies the inner and personal transformation of regeneration. In this sense, the doctrine of a regenerate church membership encapsulates all that a church is to do and to be.

Belief in a regenerate church membership affirms the necessity of the moral purity of a church. The quest to have a church that follows the biblical model is a commitment to retain the distinction between the world and the covenant community of God. Failing to emphasize regeneration as a prerequisite for church membership has historically resulted in the loss of an emphasis upon the church as a holy community and has given rise to moral corruption and heretical teachings within the fellowship. The distinctions between the redeemed and unredeemed are eventually blurred, if not lost altogether.

The importance of this doctrine cannot be overstated. The nature and mission of the church require that there is no place in the membership of a Christian congregation for the unconverted. From our understanding of this doctrine, we Baptists limit the membership in our churches to those who profess and give evidence of conversion. We believe that Scripture and reason support our position that a church is a pure spiritual body and that none but the regenerate are to be received into its membership. Because of this belief, we reject infant baptism and sacramentalism. We require a conscious profession of faith before baptism. These beliefs are the only biblical safeguards for the spirituality of the churches.

We believe that our Baptist distinctives are the biblical tenets that uphold the New Testament standard. Only churches that are spiritual in nature can accomplish the kingdom mission of God in the world. Only churches that have regenerate members fulfill the biblical ideal.

Chapter 4

CHURCH DISCIPLINE

One of the most glaring omissions in modern Baptist church life is the regular practice of biblical church discipline. The demise of this practice may well rest in the fact that, by and large, contemporary Baptists have not been taught or do not understand the concept of a New Testament church. The majority of Baptist churches today do not perceive themselves as believers joined together by the bond of the Spirit and associated by covenant in a shared confession of faith in the Lord Jesus Christ and a common fellowship of the gospel. Contemporary Baptists seem instead to understand themselves as autonomous individuals casually associated together in loose-knit groupings called churches. The concept of a spiritual accountability to God and to one another is lacking or ignored.

The neglect of church discipline as a regular and meaningful part of church life is a departure from our Baptist roots. Baptists have historically believed that church discipline was not just a matter of obedience; church health and vitality depended on it. Baptists believed that our beliefs, mission, witness, proclamation, spirituality, governance, fellowship, and morality were tied to the faithful practice of discipline.

American Baptists in the nineteenth century gave careful attention to the procedure and practice of church discipline. Baptist historian Gregory Wills notes, "To an antebellum Baptist, a church without discipline would hardly have counted as a church."[77] Baptist churches would devote entire days to dealing with disciplinary matters. Congregations would gather to heal breaches of fellowship, admonish way-ward members, rebuke the obstinate, and if required, excom-municate the unrepentant. By engaging in these activities, Baptists believed that they were following the biblical pattern established by Christ and the apostles for the health and effec-tiveness of the church.[78]

The spiritual revitalization of Baptist churches requires that we assume the mantle of obedience and once again prac-tice this important church ministry. The health of our churches will continue to suffer from a spiritual malaise and slide into moral decay and cultural accommodation until we are faithful to do what Christ has instructed us to do. New Testament churches practice church discipline. No church can genuinely claim to be a New Testament church or a Baptist church if it is unfaithful to what the Bible teaches about the practice of church discipline.

BIBLICAL TEACHING ON THE DOCTRINE OF CHURCH DISCIPLINE

The practice of church discipline is directly commanded by the Lord. In his instructions about the future church, Jesus gave his disciples the procedure for discipline. Matthew

18:15–20 is typically considered to be the most important and definitive text for church discipline. The promise of divine authority is found in verse 18 in Jesus' statement: "I assure you: Whatever you bind on earth is already bound in heaven, and whatever you loose on earth is already loosed in heaven."

Jesus used the terminology of "binding and loosing" elsewhere. In response to Peter's great confession, Jesus promised, "I will give you the keys of the kingdom of heaven, and whatever you bind on earth is already bound in heaven, and whatever you loose on earth is already loosed in heaven" (Matt. 16:19). The terms *binding* and *loosing* were concepts used by the Jewish rabbis in the first century to refer to the power of judging matters on the basis of the revelation of God. The Jewish authorities would determine how the Scriptures applied in a specific situation, and they would then render a judgment either by binding (to restrict) or by loosing (to liberate). Christ has given the church the necessary authority to restrict a sinful person under a disciplinary process or to liberate a repentant believer from the process. The church exercises discipline with the authority of heaven because the Lord is with them, providing assurance and guidance in the process.

The basis for church discipline rests on the holiness of God. God demands that his children be holy. Throughout the Bible, the people of God are characterized by his holiness. This moral purity is not their own achievement but the work of God in their midst. The New Testament describes the church as the people of God, who are to be known to the world by their purity of life and integrity of message.

Peter reminded the church of this ideal in his quotation of select Old Testament texts: "But you are a chosen race, a royal priesthood, a holy nation, a people for His possession, so that you may proclaim the praises of the One who called you out of darkness and into his marvelous light. Once you were not a people, but now you are God's people; you had not received mercy, but now you have received mercy." The apostle then admonished his readers: "Dear friends, I urge you as aliens and temporary residents to abstain from fleshly desires that war against you. Conduct yourselves honorably among the Gentiles, so that in a case where they speak against you as those who do evil, they may, by observing your good works, glorify God in a day of visitation" (1 Pet. 2:9–12).

Baptist theologian R. Albert Mohler provides commentary on the implications of this passage with the concept of church discipline.

> As the new people of God, the church is to see itself as an alien community in the midst of spiritual darkness—strangers to the world who must abstain from the lusts and enticements of the world. The church is to be conspicuous in its purity and holiness and steadfast in its confession of the faith once for all delivered to the saints. Rather than capitulating to the moral (or immoral) environment, Christians are to be conspicuous by their good behavior. As Peter summarized, "Just as he who called you is holy, so be holy in all you do" (1 Pet. 1:15).[79]

Individual believers and particular churches are therefore to be characterized by the holiness of God (Heb. 12:7–11). The church is now the sanctuary for the presence of the Holy God, his temple where his holy presence resides. God requires that his church reflect his holy character (1 Pet. 1:16). Failure to discipline indicates unwillingness on the part of the church to ensure that his character is rightly and clearly reflected. God has chosen to make his name and glory known through the church. Only a pure, holy church can radiate the glory of

God to the world. Church discipline is one means by which the holiness of the church is preserved.

The church is to practice discipline because God himself disciplines those whom he loves. Every believer as a child of God has at one time or another experienced the chastening work of God. "For the Lord disciplines the one He loves, and punishes every son whom He receives" (Heb. 12:6). As an expression of familial relationship, God disciplines those who belong to him. As an expression and reflection of this aspect of his character, God requires his church to discipline its members.

The writings of Paul reveal that the early church put into practice the instructions of the Lord. First Corinthians 5:1 recounts the incident of a man who was "living with his father's wife"—a reference to an incestuous relationship. Paul rebuked the Corinthian church for their failure to deal with the matter. In fact, Paul rebuked the church for its pride and toleration of such aberrant, sinful behavior (1 Cor. 5:2). He instructed the Corinthian believers to "turn that one over to Satan for the destruction of the flesh" (1 Cor. 5:5)—a call for the church to excommunicate the man. This process appears to have had the desired effect because 2 Corinthians 2:4–8 indicates that the apostle had to remind the congregation to forgive and comfort the repentant man and to restore him back into the fellowship.

Other passages in the New Testament also reveal instances where the early church obeyed the command of Christ and practiced church discipline. Galatians 6:1 provides instructions for restoration and cautions against pride. The church at Thessalonica was to warn and eventually withdraw from those who were lazy as well as those who rejected apostolic teaching (2 Thess. 3:6–15). Paul sent instructions to Timothy to excommunicate Hymenaeus and Alexander for blasphemy (1 Tim. 1:20). Elders or overseers who sinned were to be rebuked publicly as a warning to others (1 Tim. 5:19–20). Titus was to issue warnings to divisive people to cease from their controversial and heretical speculations. After appropriate warnings, Titus was to "reject," or withdraw, from them (Titus 3:9–11).

CHURCH DISCIPLINE IN BAPTIST THOUGHT

The identification of proper church discipline as a mark of a New Testament church dates as far back as the Reformed confession of faith, the Belgic Confession of 1561:

> The marks by which the true Church is known are these: If the pure doctrine of the gospel is preached therein; if she maintains the pure administration of the sacraments as instituted by Christ; if church discipline is exercised in punishing of sin; in short, if all things are managed according to the Word of God, all things contrary thereto rejected, and Jesus Christ acknowledged as the only Head of the Church. Hereby the true Church may certainly be known, from which no man has a right to separate himself.[80]

Church discipline and its implications for church membership were prominent emphases in the writings and practices of early Baptist and Anabaptist life. One of the oldest Anabaptist articles of faith, the Schleitheim Articles (1527) in article 2 discusses the "ban" (excommunication) as a principal point for their union to which all members must agree and submit.[81] In his treatise "The Church of God" (1560),

Dietrich Philips identified as one of the seven "ordinances" or marks of the true church "evangelical separation, without which the church of God cannot stand or be maintained."[82]

Peter Rideman addressed the issue of exclusion when he stated, "Therefore, do we watch over one another, telling each other his faults, warning and rebuking with all diligence. But where one will not accept the rebuke, but disregardeth it, the matter is brought before the Church, and if he hear not the Church, then he is excluded and put out."[83] Menno Simons wrote prolifically on church discipline.[84] John Smyth declared that Christ has granted the church the power to excommunicate and that final appeals for disciplinary matters rested with the church.[85] In his English Declaration at Amsterdam, Thomas Helwys noted,

> That Brethren impenitent in one sin after the admonition of the Church, are to bee excluded the cōmmunion off the Sainets. Mat. 18.17. 1 Cor. 5.4, 13. & therefore not the cōmmitting off sin doth cut off anie from the Church, but refusing to heare the Church to reformacion.[86]

The First London Confession of the Particular Baptists (1644) states that every member is subject to congregational discipline and that "the Church ought with great care and tenderness, with due advice to proceed against her members."[87] The Charleston Church Discipline (1774) defines three types or degrees of church censure: (1) the rebuke, admonition, or brotherly reproof; (2) suspension "from office, from the Lord's table"; and (3) excommunication, or exclusion "from union and communion with the church, and from all rights and privileges thereof."[88] Church discipline was a prominent theme in the writings of J. R. Graves and was a key factor in his argument for local church practice regarding the Lord's Supper.[89]

The Abstract of Principles of The Southern Baptist Theological Seminary (1858) identifies the three essential marks of a New Testament church as order, discipline, and worship:

> The Lord Jesus is the Head of the Church, which is composed of all His true disciples, and in Him is invested supremely all power for its government. According to His commandment, Christians are to associate themselves into particular societies or churches; and to each of these churches He hath given needful authority for administering that order, discipline and worship which He hath appointed. The regular officers of a Church are Bishops or Elders, and Deacons.[90]

The sampling of the evidence demonstrates that church discipline was regarded by our Baptist ancestors as a biblical practice. Our history also reveals that church discipline was widely practiced by the majority of Baptist churches before the twentieth century. One of the convictions of our denominational forebears was their pledge to separate themselves from the world and to submit themselves to Christ and to one another. Church discipline was considered one means of achieving this distinction.

THE OCCASION FOR DISCIPLINE

The New Testament does not explicitly state the criteria for determining which offenses are worthy of discipline or what sins could trigger the process. Although the Bible does join church discipline with the purity of the church, the biblical pattern reveals that the disciplinary process was practiced with discretion and care. The apostle Paul had much to say about the sins of the people in the church at Corinth, among which were divisiveness, sexual immorality, and disorderly conduct. But Paul instructed only the discipline of the man involved in an incestuous sexual relationship. We find this same discretionary care for church discipline exercised throughout the New Testament. No attempt is ever made to make the church sinlessly perfect by disciplining every sinful deviation or infraction.[91]

The common theme that seems to tie together the instances of church discipline in the New Testament are those sins that have a harmful, public effect upon the congregation in some way. Several categories of offense in the New Testament that require discipline include difficulties between members of a church (Matt. 18:15–17; 1 Cor. 5:5–6), disorderly conduct (2 Thess. 3:6–15), divisiveness (Rom. 16:17–18; Titus 3:9–10), and blatant immorality (1 Cor. 5:1–13).

Along with the sins of sexual immorality, Paul also lists greed, idolatry, drunkenness, abusive speech, and swindling as worthy of discipline (1 Cor. 5:11). False teaching is also identified as an offense that merits church discipline (1 Tim. 1:20; 2 Tim. 2:17–18; Rev. 2:14–16). These false teachings are not lesser or minor issues of biblical interpretation but rather involve the fundamental doctrines of the faith.[92]

All the sins that were explicitly disciplined in the New Testament appear to be publicly known or outwardly evident and probably had been occurring over a period of time. The public nature and knowledge of the sins brought reproach on the church, impugned the integrity of its message and mission, and dishonored the cause of Christ. Further, the refusal of the church to address such matters would have signaled the approval of the congregation and could have encouraged others to follow the sinful practices that were publicly tolerated in the fellowship.[93]

Without being too simplistic, we can cluster all of these various sins that are the occasion for church discipline into three main categories. These are fidelity to orthodox doctrine, purity and holiness of life, and unity of the fellowship. Each of these three areas is vitally important for the health and integrity of the faith and practice of the church.

THE PROCEDURE FOR DISCIPLINE

The first step in the discipline process is the recognition that an offense has occurred. "If your brother sins against you, go and rebuke him in private. If he listens to you, you have won your brother" (Matt. 18:15). The offended individual is first to seek reconciliation privately with the offender. If the offender recognizes his sin and repents, the offended person has won. The need for privacy is important because this limits the extent of the injury created by the sin and prevents a public confrontation that would make the problem worse.

The initial period of private confrontation may not, however, end in repentance and restoration. If this step fails to elicit reconciliation, then other members of the church are to be included in the process. "But if he won't listen, take one or two more with you, so that by the testimony of two or three witnesses every fact may be established" (Matt. 18:16).

In this verse, Jesus quoted Deuteronomy 19:15, a text which requires the testimony of multiple witnesses to establish the facts of dispute. Jesus draws on the Old Testament rule that a person may not be convicted of a crime on the basis of a single witness (Num. 35:30; Deut. 17:6; 19:15). At least two witnesses are necessary to ensure that an accusation is made with integrity, truthfulness, and in an unprejudiced manner. The inclusion of others in the process does not have the purpose of establishing the original charge (the truth of which is taken for granted). The presence of others is to bring moral pressure on the offender and to observe his attitude if it should become necessary to testify before the church.

The witnesses are to assist in the attempted restoration of the errant brother, but if the attempt fails, they will serve as witnesses, not of the original transgression but of the failure to repent. Bringing a sin to a brother's attention in the presence of witnesses is not to threaten or intimidate but to reinforce the severity of the sin and to strengthen the appeal for repentance.

If the errant church member will not listen and repent in the presence of others, then the process moves into the third phase. Jesus instructed his disciples to "tell the church" (Matt. 18:17). The leadership of the church should be included and provide direction for guiding a church to address the matter as a corporate body, following Paul's instructions that the "spiritual" are to restore those overtaken in a fault (Gal. 6:1). The public inclusion of the congregation in the process indicates that the church body is ultimately responsible for the discipline of its membership.

Offenses that merit disciplinary action are always serious. The inclusion of the entire church body, however, intensifies the severity of the situation and further strengthens the appeal for repentance. The church must discern the facts of the situation and render a judgment based on the teachings of the Word of God. The deportment of the church in this stage must always be Christlike, with the goal being the restoration of the sinning brother or sister.

Jesus provided further instructions for the church if this third step should fail to bring reconciliation and restoration. "But if he doesn't pay attention even to the church, let him be like an unbeliever and a tax collector to you" (Matt. 18:17). The church is to treat the unrepentant individual as an unbeliever. The congregation is to "withdraw fellowship" or "excommunicate" the errant individual. The separation is to be real and public.

When a brother or sister will not submit to the discipline of the church, then he or she is no longer considered a part of the church. The excommunicant is to be treated as a nonbeliever, an unregenerate person outside the community of Christ.

Just like any non-Christian, he would be welcome at a worship service (if his presence would not disturb those he may have hurt or cause other disruptions in the unity of the Spirit). Hearing the gospel proclaimed is a privilege that every unbeliever should have. But communion, fellowship, and meetings for support or ministry are closed. Since he gives no evidence of being a believer, he is to be treated as such until he repents. When the opportunity arises, the church should give witness to the individual, but Christian fellowship cannot take place until repentance and restoration first occur.

Sins that are public in nature and that impact the entire congregation are the offenses that merit the disciplinary act of the church. These include (1) divisions and factions that destroy Christian unity and fellowship; (2) moral and ethical deviations that violate purity and holiness of life; and (3) false doctrines that reject the essential tenets of the Christian faith. Although offenses in any of these categories can trigger the discipline process, the act of excommunication is exercised on those who fail to repent of their sin. The excommunicated are therefore doubly judged: (1) they are judged for their entrenchment in their sin; and (2) they are judged for their unwillingness to repent of their sin.

Although individuals and groups are involved in its various phases, church discipline is the prerogative and responsibility of the corporate body. The final act of excommunication is a corporate act of the congregation. Since the church as a body disciplines, the congregation is also to act corporately in the restoration of the repentant. The church must forgive and comfort the repentant brother as well as confirm their love toward him (2 Cor. 2:6–8).

THE PURPOSE OF CHURCH DISCIPLINE

Church discipline is the process by which a local church works to restore a professing Christian who has fallen into sin. The errant person may be the leader of an entire denomination or a low-profile member of a small rural church. All members are subject to the disciplinary action of the church.

The primary purpose of church discipline is the restoration (of the offender to right behavior and attitude) and reconciliation (between the believers and with God). Church discipline is an act of love to bring repentance and restoration in the life of the errant brother or sister. With discipline comes hope for renewal (1 Cor. 5:6–8). Sin hinders fellowship among believers and with God. Reconciliation and restoration can occur only when the church confronts and deals with the sinful offender.

A church that disciplines acts in love to reclaim a straying brother or sister, restore that person to right fellowship, and to rescue him or her from destructive patterns of life that threaten the ministry and message of the church. Even the act of excommunication is taken with the hope that the errant person will repent and be restored to the fold of God. If the church will remember the ultimate purpose for church discipline, then it will be easier for the Christians involved to act genuinely with love and concern as they participate in the disciplinary process.

Church discipline also keeps sin from spreading to the rest of the fellowship. Churches that regularly and faithfully practice biblical church discipline are following a biblical prescription that will keep sin from spreading and contaminating the rest of the fellowship. The author of Hebrews alluded to the corporate, contaminating effect of sin when he stated: "See to it that no one falls short of the grace of God and that no root of bitterness springs up, causing trouble and by it, defiling many" (Heb. 12:15). The apostle Paul mentioned this dynamic when he warned the Corinthian church: "Don't you know that a little yeast permeates the whole batch of dough? Clean out the old yeast so that you may be a new batch" (1 Cor. 5:6–7).

The sinful effects of the undisciplined may spread to others who are aware of the problem and know that the church did nothing about it. This neglect on the part of the church could cause some within the fellowship to think that sin is not as bad as they thought, thereby tempting them to commit similar sins. Church discipline helps the church avoid the contamination of sin. In fact, the public discipline of wayward elders before a congregation serves as a warning to the church to deter the members from similar sins (1 Tim. 5:20).

Church discipline also preserves the communal purity and holiness of the congregation. The Lord Jesus Christ wants to present to himself a church "in splendor, without spot or wrinkle or any such things, but holy and blameless" (Eph. 5:27). Christ is the Head of the church, and its character reflects upon its testimony of him. Even angels and demons look at the church and see the manifold wisdom of God (Eph. 3:10). Paul exhorted Christians to "walk worthy of the calling you have received" (Eph. 4:1). The moral purity and spiritual holiness of the church are to reflect the character of God to the world. When a church member continues to sin outwardly in a way that is evident to the world, Christ is dishonored and the integrity of the church's work and witness is impugned. The apostle Peter encouraged believers to "make every effort to be found in peace without spot or blemish before Him" (2 Pet. 3:14). Christians are to live in obedience to the Word of God and to be exemplary in their conduct.

THE DECLINE OF THE PRACTICE OF CHURCH DISCIPLINE

Several factors in Baptist life have contributed to the decline of the practice of church discipline in our churches. The cultural shift of the twentieth century precipitated the rise of a stringent individual autonomy. Christians have bought into the every-man-is-an-island mentality that is prevalent in our age. The absolute relativism that pervades Western secular society has managed to seep slowly but surely into our churches. As a result, the church is awash in a brash individualism that blunts its ability to make moral judgments. The common mantras of this attitude are "mind your own business" or "who are we to judge?"

Because of the reluctance of Christians to make moral judgments based on the Word of God, some of the sins that automatically led to ecclesiastical censure or possible excommunication in the past are now regarded by the church as justifiable or acceptable. The movement of the church away from communal accountability toward autonomous individualism is one factor that destroys the authority or will of a church to exercise discipline.

Another reason for the decline of church discipline results from a general lack of respect for authority within the church. The anti-institutional mood of the past four decades has eroded ecclesiastic authority. Our Baptist ancestors held a high view of the authority of the church and regarded church discipline as a grave matter. In contrast, church authority today (especially in our free church tradition) is met with skepticism and contempt. The attitude of disrespect for church and ministerial authority that is common outside the church has made significant inroads into the church. The result is that many Christians imbibe the secular disdain for authority in general and authority within the church in particular.

Differing denominational policies also contribute to the demise of church discipline. Some denominations have no guidelines for discipline. Other denominations are lax or lack the wherewithal to follow whatever rules or guidelines they may have. In addition, local congregations do not honor the disciplinary actions of sister churches. Anyone who is disciplined or censured can consequently leave one denomination or local church and join another without any difficulty. This denominational laxity reduces the effectiveness of discipline.

Confusion over Christian accountability within the local church further erodes the church's ability to discipline its members. To belong to the Lord is to belong to his church and to submit to the discipline of his people (Matt. 18:15–18; Gal. 6:1–2). But few Christians today desire or agree to be accountable to other believers. Spiritual accountability is all but nonexistent in many Baptist congregations.

Behind the cultural, philosophical, and theological factors that contribute to the deterioration of church discipline lie two fears that contribute to its decline.

The first of these fears is the loss of revenue. The potential for an "empty offering plate" is a major reason some churches will not practice discipline. Leaders in these Baptist churches fear that, if discipline were practiced, a massive exodus would ensue, leaving the church unable to meet its financial obligations. Further, the potential for a loss of tithes and contributions is particularly acute when the church must confront and possibly excommunicate its largest contributor. Of course, this attitude is a compromise of the truth and conviction of God. The local church must not be "held hostage." Baptist churches must trust the Lord to take care of their needs and obediently practice what Christ has commanded.

The second deterrent to the exercise of discipline is the rising fear of litigation. Those who practice discipline might find themselves being sued by the recipients of the church's disciplinary activity. More and more churches fear a legal backlash if they make any attempt to discipline their members. Churches should be sensitive, loving, and careful whenever it becomes necessary to discipline a member, but the church must be faithful to the biblical mandate to discipline despite the threat of potential legal action.

In response to a situation in which a church was sued by a former member, Chuck Colson noted: "It will be sad news if the court should emasculate the church by holding that it can't enforce biblical standards on its members; but it will be even worse news if it turns out that by ignoring our biblical responsibilities we have done it to ourselves."[94]

Each of these reasons poses formidable challenges to our Baptist churches in the reclamation and practice of church discipline. For that matter, every generation of Baptists has had to contend with its own unique cultural and pragmatic pressures that jeopardized its practice of church discipline.

Before the twentieth century, most Baptist churches were able to face and overcome these challenges. The twentieth century, however, witnessed the capitulation of most Southern Baptist churches to philosophical and societal pressures. Now in the twenty-first century, we must confront and overcome all challenges that threaten to undermine our fidelity to biblical church discipline. Let us move forward by returning to our roots and reclaiming church discipline as one of the true marks of a New Testament church.

CONCLUSION

In his essay "The Church: Baptists and Their Churches in the Eighteenth and Nineteenth Centuries," Gregory A. Wills recounts the story of a significant Southern Baptist leader who was subjected to the church discipline.

On October 16, 1814, William B. Johnson, one of the most respected antebellum Baptist leaders, separated from the First Baptist Church of Savannah, Georgia. He declared himself no longer their pastor, not even a member of the church, and marched out. The congregation expressed their respect and goodwill by inviting him to fill the pulpit temporarily, if he refrained from stirring the controversy between him and the church. Johnson agreed but could not resist the temptation to rebuke the church the following Sunday—he declared them a "corrupt body." For the next five years the regular Baptist churches rejected fellowship with him. . . . In 1819 William B. Johnson regained fellowship with regular Baptists when he repented of his condemnation of the

Savannah church and promised to refrain from attempts to impose his views.[95]

This episode from Baptist life illustrates three principles we have examined in our brief survey of church discipline. No Christian, no matter how prominent or esteemed, is above the discipline of the church. Also, restoration and reclamation can be achieved, and a person can be restored to meaningful ministry.

One of the convictions of early Baptists was their pledge to separate themselves from the world and to submit themselves to Christ and to one another. We would do well to follow in their footsteps. Church discipline is one means of achieving this distinction. Church discipline is an act of obedience to the teachings of Christ (Matt. 18:15–20) and is a means of preserving and facilitating fidelity to right doctrine, purity of life (holiness), and unity of fellowship.[96] Church discipline is the prerogative of a local church.

Our Baptist ancestors considered church discipline one of the marks of a true church, and they practiced it accordingly. This high regard assigned to church discipline is represented in the following statement from John Leadley Dagg: "It has been remarked, that when discipline leaves a church, Christ goes with it."[97] If such is the case, then many of our Baptist churches are in serious trouble.

As Baptists, we should seek to maintain a clear distinction between those who belong to Christ and those who belong to the world. We must instruct those who want to join our churches that their membership includes accountability to the authority of the congregation. In addition, membership in our churches should require submission of the beliefs and conduct of the individual to the judgment of the church. The gospel message will lose its integrity and power if our churches do not remain distinct from the world. Church discipline is one means of preserving the integrity and impact of the message and ministry of our Baptist churches.[98]

The doctrine of church discipline certainly is not the exclusive "theological property" of Baptists. Our contention that church discipline is a mark of a New Testament church has, however, enjoyed strong, historical support in Baptist life, especially before the twentieth century. In addition, the coupling of church discipline with the doctrines of a regenerate church membership and congregational polity gives our understanding and practice of church discipline a distinctively Baptist perspective.

Chapter 5

CONGREGATIONAL POLITY

In September 2004, I attended a meeting of various SBC leaders to discuss matters related to denominational and church polity. Our conversation focused in particular on developing church planting-ecclesiological strategies that were both biblical and Baptist. Everyone in attendance believed that the church-planting strategies of our denominational entities should reflect the beliefs of Southern Baptists. Our primary concern was to establish broad guidelines that would assist one of our Southern Baptist missions agencies in its task of church planting.[99]

All those in attendance realized the importance and implications of our discussion. Numerous items were discussed and debated. Although the climate of the meeting was cordial and fraternal, deeply held convictions were occasionally articulated with great intensity. After several hours of dialogue, a consensus of positions acceptable to all began to emerge. As a means of bringing our session to a close, the facilitator of the meeting went to each person in the meeting to solicit final comments and opinions. Finally, the last person addressed by the facilitator, who had said very little during the entire discussion, was asked, "Do you have any final comments or observations?"

His response, which was both humorous and insightful, can be paraphrased as follows: "When I first was asked to attend this meeting to discuss Baptist polity, I thought it would be about as exciting as watching paint dry. But after several hours of listening to our discussion, I now see that Baptist polity is incredibly important and has profound implications for the ministry of our churches and our denomination."

This man's remarks reflect the attitudes of many Baptists today. Few Baptists pay attention to matters of church polity. Generally, polity can be defined as "the organization or government structure of a local church or fellowship of churches,"[100] or more simply as "a form of church government adopted by an ecclesiastical body."[101] Polity involves governance and organization. Church polity, and for Baptists, congregational polity, is the way a local church organizes and administrates its ministries in the quest of its mission. Understood in this way, church polity is quite important.

DEFINING CONGREGATIONAL POLITY

Baptists have historically believed that congregational church polity is important. Although not an essential of the Christian faith, Baptists have contended that the New Testament has established the manner in which a local church is to govern and administrate itself. Since these Baptists believed that the New Testament has fixed the pattern of polity, they were not at liberty to govern themselves in any fashion. If Christ has established the laws of church government, they were obligated to follow the dictates of the Head and Lord of the church.

Three major expressions of church polity exist within Christendom. One type of polity is the form of Episcopal church government. Episcopal church polity locates ultimate authority for decision making in the office of the bishop. Power for decision making may reside with a single bishop, such as the pope in Roman Catholicism, or it may reside in a group of bishops. Another form of church polity is Presbyterianism. The decision making power in this structure resides in a group of elders. In the local church, this group forms the session. Select elders (or presbyters) from various churches in a certain geographical area form a presbytery. A third expression of church polity is Congregationalism. This form of church governance emphasizes the autonomy, independence, and authority of the local church. The ultimate authority for decision making resides within the gathered congregation.[102]

The vast majority of Baptists have historically practiced congregational church polity. "From their beginnings Baptists have espoused Congregational polity."[103] Congregational polity may be defined as "that form of church governance in which final human authority rests with the local or particular congregation when it gathers for decision-making. This means that decisions about membership, leadership, doctrine, worship, conduct, missions, finances, property, relationships, and the like are to be made by the gathered congregation except when such decisions have been delegated by the congregation to individual members or groups of members."[104]

The intention of congregational polity is that the congregation govern itself under the lordship of Jesus Christ and the leadership of the Holy Spirit, under the delegated authority of pastors and deacons, but with no governing ecclesial bodies exerting authority over the church. All members participate in the decision-making process.[105] The congregational polity of a church embodies democratic processes, is responsible to the lordship of Jesus Christ, and is guided by his authoritative word, the inerrant Scriptures.[106]

Every believer has the same right and equal access to God through Christ. Hierarchical distinctions between clergy and laity are foreign and repugnant to the Baptist conception of the church. Each believer is responsible for seeking direction and wisdom from the Holy Spirit and expressing his convictions within the decision-making structures of the local church. This aversion to hierarchical relationships among the members within a Baptist church also translates to the relationships among Baptist churches. Each local church is independent from all other ecclesiastical structures or authorities; all Baptist churches are equal.[107]

The word *democracy* has been used throughout much of Baptist life to describe congregational polity, and the concept is often associated with the decision-making processes that occur within Baptist churches. In a qualified sense, our Baptist churches are "democratic" in that each member is equal to every other member with regard to the spiritual blessings of salvation and justified standing before God. Further, every believer has the same, direct access to God through Christ as any other Christian. Each member also has the potential to participate appropriately in the decision-making process as any other member.

In their relation to the Lord of the church, however, Baptist churches are not "democratic." Christ's will and authority are absolute in our churches. One Baptist leader has stated that each congregation "must be subject to his [Jesus

Christ's] will as revealed in the New Testament and as experienced under the guidance of the Holy Spirit. The Lord has left, however, a large range of initiatives to the churches as they are led by the Holy Spirit and as they keep within the boundaries of the New Testament principles. This is particularly true as to methods."[108]

BIBLICAL TEACHING ON CONGREGATIONAL POLITY

Baptists today find themselves struggling with the question, "Does the Bible teach congregational church polity?" The following brief survey will demonstrate that the Scriptures do in fact support the Baptist position on church governance.

MATTHEW 18:15–20

As already noted in the previous chapter, this passage is the primary text for our understanding of church discipline. Matthew is the only Gospel to use the term *church*. The majority of Baptist commentators understand this use of *ekklesia* to mean a local or particular church.[109] More than likely, the immediate application is to the assembly of disciples gathered around Jesus, but the larger principle anticipates the New Testament church that would be fully birthed by the Holy Spirit at Pentecost (Acts 2).[110] In his instructions for the disciplinary process, Jesus placed the final court of appeal and the act of excommunication in the church body. Each member is to abide by the corporate judgment rendered by the church.[111] As Mark Dever notes: "Notice to whom one finally appeals in such situations. What court has the final word? It is not a bishop, a pope, or a presbytery; it is not an assembly, a synod, a convention, or a conference. It is not even a pastor or a board of elders, a board of deacons or a church committee. It is, quite simply, the church—that is, the assembly of those individual believers who are the church."[112]

ACTS 6:1–7

This passage documents the serious problem of the benevolent distribution of food. The widows of the Hebraic Jews were receiving daily distribution of the allotted meals, while the widows of the Hellenistic Jews were being overlooked. Two issues were of particular concern: How would the daily distribution of food take place, and who would be responsible for this task? The presence of the apostle makes the manner of resolution even more astounding. In Acts 6:2, the apostles acknowledged that they must continue in what they had been commissioned by God to do—"preaching about God." They instructed the church in Acts 6:3 to "select from among you seven men of good reputation . . . whom we can appoint to this duty." The proposal pleased the church (Acts 6:5); they thus proceeded and selected seven men. After their selection, the church had them "stand before the apostles, who prayed and laid their hands on them" (Acts 6:6).

Although the apostles were present, the manner in which the issue was addressed and resolved was congregational. The apostles looked to the church to assume ownership of this issue and resolve the problem. The entire congregation had the responsibility to identify those who were qualified to perform this ministry. The apostles recognized and affirmed that the gathered church has the authority under Christ's lordship to oversee its own ministries. "It almost seems that they were recognizing in the church assembly the same kind of authority, under God, that Jesus had recognized in His statement in Matthew 18:15–17."[113]

Acts 13:2–3

Acts 13:2–3, which marks the beginning of Paul's first missionary journey, states: "As they were ministering to the Lord and fasting, the Holy Spirit said, 'Set apart for Me Barnabas and Saul for the work that I have called them to.' Then, after they had fasted, prayed, and laid hands on them, they sent them off." In the midst of their worship before God, the Holy Spirit likely spoke through the prophets of the church mentioned in Acts 13:1. Luke stated that the Holy Spirit's instructions were directed to the entire church at Antioch. Through these prophets, the Holy Spirit instructed the entire congregation to "set apart" or "separate" Barnabas and Saul for a particular ministry. The setting apart implies separation from the rest of the church and to another extraordinary work—the mission to the Gentiles.[114]

Scholars are divided on exactly who performed the laying on of hands mentioned in Acts 13:3. One interpretation suggests that only Simeon, Niger, Lucius, and Manaen laid hands on Barnabas and Saul. Another interpretation claims that the entire congregation participated in the action. Regardless of which position is adopted, the overall context suggests that the ultimate responsibility and the oversight for the "setting apart" activities rested with the entire church. Even if the four men were the only ones who laid hands on Barnabas and Saul, they did so under the auspices of and as representatives of the entire congregation. The laying on of hands served as an act of consecration and commissioning of the two for the Gentile mission.

Acts 15

The significance of this passage cannot be overstated for the direction of the gospel in the early church. The church at

Antioch sent a theological inquiry to the church at Jerusalem. A council was convened by Paul, Barnabas, and other representatives at Jerusalem in order to determine whether Gentile converts must be circumcised and observe the Mosaic Law in order to be saved. Pharisaic Christians argued that the Gentiles had to be circumcised, but Peter countered that the giving of the Holy Spirit to these converts indicated that God made no distinction between the Jewish and Gentile Christians. In addition, Paul and Barnabas gave testimony to God's mighty work among the Gentile believers. James did not believe that the Gentiles had to observe Mosaic rituals in order to be Christians. Therefore, he made a fourfold proposal to resolve the dispute: "abstain from things polluted by idols, from sexual immorality, from eating anything that has been strangled, and from blood" (Acts 15:20).

This passage has profound implications for local church autonomy, voluntary cooperation among churches, and congregationalism. Daniel Akin identifies six important ecclesiological issues that impact our understanding of church polity.

First, the local church at Antioch sent Paul and Barnabas to Jerusalem (Acts 15:2–3), and the local church at Jerusalem, along with the apostles and other leaders, received them (Acts 15:4).

Second, the Antioch church appears to have initiated the conference between Paul and Barnabas, the apostles and elders, and other Jerusalem representatives about the Gentile issue. In other words, the church initiated the activity, not the apostles or other leaders.

Third, although the apostles and elders convened and led the session, the entire church "listened" to the debate (Acts 15:12).

Fourth, the entire church, along with the apostles and elders, "decided to select men from among them and to send them to Antioch with Paul and Barnabas" (Acts 15:22) to deliver the decision reached by the Jerusalem Council. Among those selected were Judas Barsabbas and Silas.

Fifth, the letter was directed to the entire churches at Antioch, Syria, and Cilicia (Acts 15:23).

Sixth, the entire church at Antioch received the letter and corporately rejoiced over its encouragement (Acts 15:30–31).

As Akin notes, "In all that took place congregational involvement and action are present at every turn."[115] Throughout the process, no hierarchy was developed, and no dictates were issued by church officials. The Jerusalem and Antioch congregations were involved in all deliberations and decisions.

1 CORINTHIANS 5:4–5

Once again the issue of church discipline arises. The responsibility for the discipline of the man involved in sexual immorality resided with the entire congregation ("when you are assembled," 1 Cor. 5:4). Paul instructed the entire church, not simply the leaders, to excommunicate the man. The apostle was disturbed that the Corinthians were tolerating this sin instead of removing its presence from their midst. As J. W. MacGorman pointed out, that disciplinary action "was the responsibility of the entire congregation rather than that of the leadership only (v. 4). This was not the kind of problem that could be turned over to a committee for resolution. It was a body problem, not simply an arm or leg problem, and it required the participation of all members."[116]

2 CORINTHIANS 2:6

The matter of church discipline again provides the context for congregational action. The man mentioned in this verse was apparently involved in a serious sin (likely the same man mentioned in 1 Cor. 5:1). He apparently, however, had repented of the sin. Second Corinthians 2:6 states: "The punishment by the majority is sufficient for such a person." The text suggests that the Corinthian church acted formally and judicially against the offender. David Garland observes: "Paul's concern about the punishment of the offender presents the picture that church members presided as judges over the person involved and pronounced a sentence."[117] In order for a majority to be established, the church evidently invoked some form of adjudication, possibly even a vote.[118]

Certain New Testament texts either teach or model congregational polity. I consider the texts discussed above to be the most significant evidence in support of congregationalism. Other passages that equally support or allude to this form of polity are Acts 11:22; 14:27; 1 Corinthians 7–12; 16:3–4; and 2 Corinthians 6.

Some passages in the New Testament are not as clear as we would like in their depictions of church governance. Other passages are, however, more explicit in their teachings and, in my estimation, fully support congregational polity. As we have seen in our biblical survey, Congregationalism is typically associated with other ecclesiastical matters or practices. These include church discipline and the commissioning (ordaining?) or consecrating of church leaders for certain ministry or missional tasks.

CONGREGATIONAL POLITY AND BAPTIST IDENTITY

Baptists have historically understood congregational polity to be part of our distinctive theological identity. This fact is clearly and unequivocally supported in writings on Baptist distinctives.[119] For example, J. B. Gambrell noted that the "New Testament ecclesiastical unit is a local church." Each church is independent of and autonomous from every other church. All ecclesiastical authority is vested in each particular congregation. "The churches are wholly dependent on their Head and subject to His law, but independent of each other and of all other bodies whatsoever."[120] Every church is directly related and subjected only to the Head of the church, Jesus Christ. Baptists believe that New Testament churches "were local, independent, and self-governing bodies."

B. H. Carroll likewise embodied the same sentiments of the majority of Baptists. He noted that the church is a "pure democracy." As a democracy, each local congregation is responsible to manage its own affairs under the lordship of Christ. The ministers and members of a specific church are equal in status before God, and all share in the task and responsibility of discerning the will of God for the congregation.[121]

THE PRIESTHOOD OF ALL BELIEVERS

Baptist considerations of congregational polity typically include, in one way or another, the doctrine of the priesthood of all believers. The essential function of a priest is to stand and represent the interests and concerns of another. The concept of priesthood is integral to both the Old Testament and New Testament and finds its fulfillment in the Jesus Christ, who is the Mediator and Great High Priest. According to the doctrine of the priesthood of all believers, every believer has direct access to God through Jesus Christ, and the church is a fellowship of priests serving together under the lordship of Christ.

During the Old Testament times, it was necessary that a special priesthood be chosen by God to represent the nation of Israel before him. The priestly ministry was assigned to the tribe of Levi through the Aaronic line of descent (Exod. 40:13; Num. 1:47–54). According to this model, the priest fulfilled a representative function, entering the Holy of Holies on the Day of Atonement and making a sacrificial offering on behalf of the people. The entire nation of Israel was called a "kingdom of priests" at Sinai (Exod. 19:6) and is yet destined to function as a priestly body (Isa. 61:6). In contrast to Israel, the entire church stands as a royal priesthood, a priestly fellowship belonging to the King and sharing his glory.

Whereas the priests in the Old Testament could enter into God's presence in the Holy of Holies only once a year, the church as a priesthood has permanent access to God through its High Priest. In the Old Testament, a thick evil separated the people from God's presence. That veil was rent in two, however, by the atoning sacrifice of Jesus Christ. Christ's death on the cross is described as a priestly act that has paid the penalty of sin once for all. As a priest, Jesus did not take the blood of a representative animal into the Holy of Holies but instead entered "the greater and more perfect tabernacle" and shed his own blood to obtain "eternal redemption" (Heb. 9:11–12). Christ has fulfilled the representative role of the priesthood and is the one Mediator between God and men (1 Tim. 2:5). There is no longer a need for a human priest to stand and represent other humans before God. Believers can now enter with confidence into the holy place through Jesus Christ (Heb. 10:19–21).

The church, as a priesthood of believers, is now encouraged to "draw near" into the very presence of God. Whereas all nations had priests to perform representative functions, the church has none. The church *is* a priesthood. Although others brought sacrifices that they might approach God, the church brings none but instead approaches boldly through the finished sacrifice of Christ, its great High Priest.

Of particular significance to the doctrine of the priesthood of all believers is the concept of the gathered church, or congregationalism. Each church is comprised of believers who have been redeemed by Christ and now serve together as priests. This doctrine refers to believers gathered together under the lordship of Christ, not to individual believers serving God alone. As the people of God, the church is now a "royal priesthood" (1 Pet. 2:9) and ministers corporately in the name of Christ.

The priests in the Old Testament had three broad areas of responsibility: (1) sacrifice, the service at the altar; (2) witness, the service of proclaiming God's revelation; and (3) intercession. The New Testament reveals that the church has the same priestly functions.

The priesthood of the church makes no sacrifice for sin since Christ has offered "one sacrifice for sins forever" (Heb. 10:12). The priesthood of the church has no physical temple in which to reside and minister. Yet the New Testament priesthood, like the Old Testament priesthood, performs three broad areas of service.

The first category of service is *sacrifice.* This includes the self-sacrifice of the believer (Rom. 12:1; Phil. 2:17), the sacrifice of praise (Heb. 13:15), the sacrifice of good works (Heb. 13:16), and the sacrifice of new converts (Rom. 15:16).

A second category of service is *witness.* The church has the responsibility of being God's witness to the world. The apostle Peter says that a primary purpose of New Testament priests is to "proclaim the praises of the One who called you out of darkness into His marvelous light" (1 Pet. 2:9). The church performs this priestly ministry by proclaiming the message of the gospel as ambassadors of Christ (2 Cor. 5:20) and by living a holy life before the world (1 Pet. 2:12). The priests are to consider the church as a temple in which to perform their priestly acts so that the glory and holiness of the God who resides in his temple can be displayed (1 Cor. 6:19).

The third area of service for the New Testament priesthood is *intercession*. All the members of the priesthood have equal access to God through Christ. Intercessory prayers are to be offered for one another. This intercessory service is the responsibility both for individual priests and for the priesthood. Intercession is to be made for physical needs (Acts 12:5, 12; James 5:14–18), missionary activity (Acts 13:3), and for the spiritual needs of the church (Acts 14:23; Eph. 1:16–23; 3:14–21). The priesthood of believers is also to intercede for those outside the faith (Acts 7:60; Rom. 10:1; 1 Tim. 2:1–2).

As is evident from this overview, the priesthood of all believers has implications for our understanding for the ministry of the church. In Baptist life, the priesthood of believers is rightly associated with congregational polity, but the association is often misarticulated or misunderstood. Rightly understood, this doctrine affirms that the church as a priesthood can enter corporately into God's presence to seek and discern his will for the church.

Misinterpretations and misunderstandings of this doctrine abound in Baptist life. For example, some Baptists reason, "Because I am my own priest, I can do whatever I want" or "Because I am my own priest, I can interpret the Bible to mean whatever I want it to say, and no one can tell me otherwise." In addition, the priesthood of all believers is often misused to justify stringent individualism, irresponsible (even heretical) interpretations of Scripture, abandonment of corporate accountability, and theological anarchy.

Further, the priesthood of believers is regularly confused with soul competency and religious freedom. Baptists have and do affirm that each individual has the capacity to know and relate to God (soul competency). Through the centuries Baptists have been leaders for religious liberty, and they continue to be. Although soul competency, religious liberty, and the priesthood of all believers are interrelated, they are not identical theological concepts. As I have already shown, a New Testament understanding of the priesthood of believers dispels such erroneous ideas.

Misunderstandings of the priesthood of all Christians often lead to misstatements of the concept. I commonly hear or read some Baptists who speak of "the priesthood of the believer." This phrase attempts to wed a corporate/plural concept (priesthood) with a singular entity (the believer). The result is a confusing, nonsensical statement that conveys nothing of theological value. The biblical concept is correctly stated as "the priesthood of all believers," with the emphasis on the church's functioning collectively as believer-priests. The doctrine of the priesthood of believers cannot and should not serve as a basis for autonomous individualism or doctrinal infidelity. "Priesthood of all believers has more to do with the believer's service than with an individual's position or status."[122] To use the doctrine of the priesthood of all believers as a means to justify an overemphasis on individual experience and private biblical interpretation is to "truncate and pervert what Luther and the other Reformers intended when they formulated the doctrine of the spiritual priesthood of all believers."[123]

The priesthood of all believers does have connotations for our understanding of congregational polity. The church as a priesthood means that the congregation jointly seeks and discerns God's will for their corporate mission. The ultimate goal of the priesthood is the joint service of all believers in unified mission to a lost world.

Timothy George, in his masterful essay "The Priesthood of All Believers" states that the priesthood of all believers means

> in the community of saints, God has so tempered the body that we are all priests to each other. We stand before God and intercede for one another, we proclaim God's Word to one another and celebrate His presence among us in worship, praise, and fellowship. Moreover, our priestly ministry does not terminate upon ourselves. It propels us into the world in service and witness. It constrains us to "shew forth the praises of him who has called [us] out of darkness into his marvelous light" (1 Pet. 2:9).[124]

Congregational polity is consistent with this perspective of the priesthood of all believers and is the best way to affirm and practice this important ecclesiastical doctrine.

CONGREGATIONAL POLITY AND SANCTIFICATION

The New Testament contains several passages which indicate that spiritual growth is an expectation for local churches. Paul noted that God has gifted his church with spiritual leaders "for the training of the saints in the work of ministry, to build up the body of Christ, until we all reach unity in the faith and in the knowledge of God's Son, growing into a mature man with a stature measured by Christ's fullness" (Eph. 4:12–13). The apostle also thanked God for the Thessalonian believers because their faith was flourishing and the love of members of the church for one another was increasing (2 Thess. 1:3).

Peter encouraged the churches who received his epistle to "desire the unadulterated spiritual milk, so that you may grow by it in your salvation" (1 Pet. 2:2). The apostle also exhorted his readers to "grow in the grace and knowledge of our Lord and Savior Jesus Christ" (2 Pet. 3:18). Failure to grow (mature) from milk to solid food brings spiritual rebuke (Heb. 5:11–14).

These and similar passages suggest that sanctification is a congregational as well as an individual matter. That is, as individual believers are to grow in faith and holiness, so also are individual churches to mature corporately. Although congregational sanctification does require and assume the spiritual growth and vitality of its individual members, corporate sanctification is not simply the collective growth of each believer. Corporate sanctification is the spiritual maturation of the church as a corporate body. If each local church is a living organism that has spiritual life and health, then the dynamics of growth and maturity likewise apply to it. The Holy Spirit works in the life of each congregation to mature it in all facets of ecclesiastical life.

I believe that congregational polity is best suited to facilitate both corporate and individual sanctification. With regard to individual spiritual growth, congregational polity requires (in theory) each member to practice spiritual disciplines in order to function spiritually in the life of the church. Part of a believer's spiritual development can be his appropriate participation in the decision-making process. "By serving on committees, work groups, or ministry teams as well as by sharing in congregational meetings, wherein all members are seeking the mind and will of Christ, believers can grow in faith and understanding and in love and fellowship."[125]

With regard to corporate maturity, congregational polity likewise requires (in theory) each church to seek intentionally as a corporate body the will of God on matters related to the church. In other words, congregational polity can facilitate the membership of a church to gather collectively to discern the will of God about matters that affect the whole. The emphasis is therefore directed on matters related to the church, not on the individual.

Further, the act of discerning the will of God has a maturing impact. In other words, the process of a church's struggling together before God can have as much value as the eventual resolution of a problem or the discovery of direction or purpose. Through the shared acts of praying, studying, discussing, deliberating, and deciding, the members of a church are bonded together in a process by which they strive collectively to reach unity in the faith and growth toward maturity.

UNITY AND ORDER

Contrary to our contemporary practices, the polity structures of the congregations in the New Testament were to promote unity and order within the churches. In John 17:21, Jesus in his high priestly prayer asked that "the world may believe" through the unity of his disciples that the Father had sent him. The manner in which the disciples related to one another and corporately conducted their affairs could be considered an extension of a polity that proclaimed the mission of the Son of God.

Two women in the church at Philippi, Euodia and Syntyche, experienced a personal yet public disagreement. Paul called on the entire church to assist in the resolution of the conflict, thereby restoring unity (Phil. 4:1–3). Additionally, the church at Corinth struggled with problems of disorder and confusion in their public worship. Paul instructed the entire congregation to address the matter so everything would "be done decently and in order" (1 Cor. 14:40).

MINISTRY

As Baptists, we, along with most evangelicals, believe that God has equipped every believer with "spiritual giftings" to perform the ministry tasks to which he has called us.[126] In addition, God has equipped every church with "spiritual giftings" to achieve the mission given to them. I contend that certain manifestations of these spiritual giftings are best exercised in a polity that is congregational. Among these types of giftings are wisdom, knowledge, distinguishing between spirits, discernment, and possibly shepherding and teaching (Eph. 4:11). If these giftings are to be used as Paul instructed for the common good (1 Cor. 12:7), then congregational polity provides the best context to facilitate the exercise of these gifts in the corporate ministry of the church.[127]

CONGREGATIONAL POLITY AND PASTORAL LEADERSHIP

Congregational polity does not preclude strong, biblical pastoral leadership. In fact, as previously noted, congregational polity actually provides the best context for the gifts of leadership to function. This is true for pastoral leadership. Baptist history is certainly filled with countless examples of the abuse of pastoral authority. Baptist life, however, also has numerous examples of abusive or carnal decisions made by congregations. Because of these abuses, we do not want to overreact theologically and discount the fact that the Bible teaches both pastoral leadership and congregational polity.

The challenge for Baptists is to keep both congregational polity and pastoral leadership in their proper balance. We must walk a fine line to avoid emphasizing one of these at the expense of the other. An overemphasis on congregational decision making can lead a church to ignore the leadership and wisdom of its God-called and God-given pastor. In fact, to ignore pastoral leadership is to disparage the pastor as a gift of God to the church.

In addition, a church that will not follow the pastor or will not allow their pastor to lead disregards and discounts the appropriate expression of one of the two offices of the church—the office of overseer (1 Tim. 3:1–7). Likewise, for a pastor to exercise his leadership in an authoritarian manner is to ignore the teachings of Scripture on the appropriate inclusion and participation of the congregation in certain decisions.

Pastoral leadership is servant leadership, following the model of our Lord. Jesus was compassionate and tenderhearted in his leadership. He was also resolute, determined, and unwavering in his mission. He sacrificed himself in service to others as directed by the Father and in submission to the Holy Spirit. The example of our Lord should be the manner in which pastoral leadership is expressed.

Congregational polity is biblically supported. In addition, congregational polity facilitates ministry, witness, unity, and order in the church. Congregationalism also allows for strong pastoral leadership. Yet this form of church governance is flexible enough to allow a church to address issues that are unique to its situation. Despite all these advantages, though, "It is still possible to get the structure right and still miss the mark if the Spirit of Christ is absent."[128]

> Even the best form of church government is an empty shell if these principles [Christ's headship, the church as the organic life of his body, and the principles of service and stewardship guiding the leadership] do not grip the hearts of those who lead and those who follow. Better by far are imperfect structures in the hands of devoted servants than the most biblical form of church government practiced in pride or in a loveless and vindictive spirit.[129]

AUTONOMY

The Baptist Faith and Message (2000) describes local churches as "autonomous" because this principle is believed to reflect the basic New Testament position on church government. The primary focus in Acts and the Epistles is the local church. The Bible makes no reference to any entity exerting authority above or beyond the local church. No instance of control over a local church by outside organizations or individuals is found. The apostles made recommendations and gave advice, but they exercised no rulership or control. Even Paul had to argue for his apostolic authority and implore his readers to follow his teachings (Gal. 1:11–24).[130]

Autonomy means that each local church is self-governing. Each congregation makes its own decisions about all facets of church life, including personnel, finances, building and grounds, and other matters. A local congregation may choose to seek counsel from other churches and denominational officials, but the membership is not required or bound to follow this advice. The decisions of a local church do not require outside ratification or approval.[131]

The autonomy of the local church means that each congregation can choose for itself how to relate to other congregations. A church may practice "independent congregational polity" in which it chooses "not to associate on a sustained basis with other congregations or to affiliate with and support denominational . . . bodies for missionary, educational, benevolent, or other purposes." A congregation may practice "cooperative congregational polity" by freely associating "with other congregations 'of like faith and order' and to support denominational bodies for missionary, educational, benevolent, or other purposes."[132]

The New Testament presents churches that are independent and self-governing. The decisions of each local church are final because no authority higher than a local church exists. Local churches can join together for certain ministry, educational, or benevolent endeavors, but these shared ventures occur because of the bond of a common faith and ministry. No church assumes any authority over another church in these joint, cooperative efforts.[133] Because each church is self-governing, the congregation controls its own membership. Churches can withdraw fellowship from members for biblical cause, and they can equally restore members to fellowship upon repentance.

Autonomy also shapes the internal structures of a congregation. Churches may choose to organize themselves in structures such as the pastor and deacons, the pastor-deacons-committees, or the pastor-deacons-committees-church council. Some Baptists contend that congregational polity permits a plural elder-led polity structure.[134] In each of these cases, the internal structures are subject to the final authority of the congregation.

THE GOAL OF CONGREGATIONAL POLITY

The ultimate goal of congregation polity is for each church to discern and follow the will of the Lord of the church. With this in mind, certain qualifications of congregational polity should preclude some of the abuses often associated with this form of church governance.

First, congregational polity does not mean that the church votes on the will of God. The goal is to ascertain what is the will of God and then to obey him. Congregational polity ideally should mature the believers as they participate corporately in the governing process.

Second, congregational polity does not mean that the majority rules. Although there may be a majority, if the vote is contrary to the will of God, the congregation walks in disobedience. Rather, the goal is for the direct rule of Christ to be manifested within the congregation. Congregational polity is the attempt of Baptist churches to realize this Christocracy and to submit themselves to his rule.[135]

IMPLICATIONS

I am concerned that many Baptists today neither appreciate nor care that we are moving away from this distinctive of our Baptist identity. Several reasons seem to precipitate this move away from congregational polity.

First, some Baptists today reject congregational polity in reaction to the wrongful practice of this form of church governance in Baptist life. Some of my students share with me that they are open to adopting other forms of church polity because, according to their understanding, congregational polity creates a culture in which church conflicts can erupt, especially in a Baptist business meeting. Numerous pastors have shared with me their aversion to Congregationalism because of the abuse they have suffered from church members, all under the auspices of congregational polity. Sadly, many churches have used this form of polity to create a culture of conflict within a church or to justify their ungodly actions against a minister. Both groups (pastors and students) assume that if they adopt another form of church polity, they will insulate themselves from congregational abuse or defuse the potential for church conflicts.

I typically respond that the polity is not the problem; the problem is carnal individuals taking ungodly actions against others. Other polity structures have their own unique ways in which church leaders can suffer mistreatment or conflict can occur. Changing one's polity does not eliminate unjust treatment or church conflict; it simply changes the form and context in which it is expressed. The potential for abuse and conflict is no reason to reject what I believe is the polity taught in the Bible.

Another reason people reject congregational polity is a concern for more efficient decision making in church life. Those who advocate this reasoning do so on the premise that congregationalism is unwieldy, cumbersome, and inefficient. If the ultimate goal of polity is to render a decision, so the argument goes, then other structures of governance are more efficient. Congregationalism becomes an impediment to decision making.

I believe that church governance is intended to provide order and structure in decision making and ministry endeavors. But I do not believe that expediency and efficiency are the determining criteria for decision making. In fact, I have already suggested that there can be great spiritual value in the process of a congregation making a decision. By removing ultimate earthly authority from a local congregation and placing it in the hands of one or a few, we may eliminate an important ecclesiastical structure that facilitates corporate sanctification. In this scenario, a local church is denied a biblical structure intended to facilitate corporate spiritual growth. The church thereby never attains congregational maturity.

A third reason some Baptists abandon congregational polity is that they are convinced another form of polity is more biblical. The polity arguments of non-Baptist pastors and theologians have convinced some people that congregational polity is unbiblical or theologically unsound. Some Baptists come to this conclusion after a careful, conscientious study of all the biblical texts and theological arguments pertinent to this subject. If my interaction with pastors, church members, and students is an indication of what is happening in the broad spectrum of Baptist life, however, many Baptists abandon congregational polity because they have not seriously considered the biblical and theological arguments for Congregationalism.

Part of this dilemma stems from the fact that our Baptist distinctives are no longer regularly taught and preached in our Baptist churches. The result is a loss of understanding among our church members of the biblical basis for our Baptist beliefs. We must remind those Baptists who are contemplating other polity structures that Congregationalism is biblically sound and theologically coherent. Our Baptist ancestors articulated their polity and defended it from the critical observations and attacks of others with sound, doctrinal arguments. We should follow their example.

The biblical texts surveyed in this chapter are some of the primary passages that are foundational to our polity; we are not lacking a biblical rationale for Congregationalism. We must do a better job of teaching the biblical and theological foundations for our ecclesiastical beliefs.

CONCLUSION

Congregational polity is one of the distinctive theological tenets of Baptists. We strive to implement a church polity that is based on the New Testament, and we are convinced that Congregationalism is the most faithful to Scripture. In this paradigm, each member shares equally with the other members in the overall decisions and affairs of the church. The teaching of the New Testament prohibits hierarchical distinctions between clergy and laity. Each Baptist church is autonomous, and no church can exert ecclesiastical control or authority over another Baptist church.

Congregational polity is, in a sense, the practical application of certain other New Testament beliefs and practices. For example, congregational polity assumes the doctrine of a regenerate church membership and the practice of biblical church discipline. The glaring omission of these two crucial biblical doctrines in many Baptist congregations is a guarantee of the absence of true spirituality and the rise of ungodliness in the corporate decision-making structures of the church. The conflicts and abuses often associated with congregational polity are indictments that we have drifted from our Baptist distinctives. In addition, congregational polity best expresses the lordship of Christ.

Every form of polity other than Congregationalism is an infringement on the direct lordship of Jesus Christ. The New Testament knows nothing of a mediated lordship. E. Y. Mullins declared:

> There is no indirect lordship known to the New Testament. An ecclesiastical monarchy with a human head, like the Roman Catholic Church, radically alters the very nature of Christianity. Baptist congregationalism is the exact antithesis of the Romish hierarchy. Modified ecclesiastical monarchies, or aristocracies, or oligarchies, are less objectionable, but they too violate one or the other of the organic laws of the church, the direct lordship of Christ, or the equality of all believers in spiritual privilege.[136]

As Baptists, we believe that congregational polity is the form of church governance most faithful to the New Testament. We also believe that our polity best exemplifies what we believe are the essential values of a church, among which are the lordship of Christ, a regenerate church membership, and church discipline. Congregational polity, therefore, assists New Testament churches in their kingdom mission.

Chapter 6

RELATED CHURCH CONCERNS

The chapters that precede and follow this one relate to the distinctive theological identity of Baptists. Only one matter that we will discuss in this section (church covenant) could possibly be considered a Baptist distinctive. Most of the topics addressed, however, are not uniquely Baptist.

The reason for the inclusion of this material is twofold.

First, all the subjects examined are related to the doctrine of the church. Ecclesiastical matters are by nature organic; it is difficult to address our Baptist distinctives without discussing these related matters.

Second, certain constituencies in Baptist life are either ignoring some of these concepts (church covenant) or are intentionally redefining them (offices of the church). This appears to be the case particularly in Southern Baptist life. When we modify our distinctive theological identity, we are in essence redefining ourselves as something other than Baptists.

Although this book is primarily about Baptist distinctives, I believe our appreciation for and understanding of our Baptist identity will be enriched and strengthened by a brief examination of these subjects. The topics addressed in this chapter are the marks of a true church, the definition of a local and universal church, the church covenant, offices of a New Testament church, and the mission of the church.

Third, most of the discussion of this chapter is addressed specifically to the Southern Baptist Convention. As a Southern Baptist, I will speak to some matters that I believe are becoming more problematic within our denomination. I will occasionally refer to our confessional statement, the Baptist Faith and Message (2000), in order to speak to matters immediately pertinent to SBC life.

CLASSIC MARKS OF A TRUE CHURCH

During the patristic period, certain characteristics were developed to identify the true church. These "marks" were considered necessary to distinguish the true Christian church from heretical or schismatic groups. These traits were unity, holiness, catholicity, and apostolicity. The Roman Catholic Church has used these marks for centuries as a way to distinguish itself from other Christian groups.

Baptists and other Protestant groups have sought to use these marks with alternative interpretations. Unity of the church is defined as the oneness of the fellowship of Christians as they jointly submit to Christ and as the Spirit joins them together in the bonds of love. Holiness points to "set-apartness" for service and worship as opposed to sinless perfection of church members. Catholicity refers to the ultimate oneness of all God's children in the final state. Apostolicity underscores the commitment of a church to submit to the teachings of the apostles as contained in the Scriptures.[137]

During the Reformation, the question of what constituted the marks of a true church arose again. In particular, Protestants began to ask whether the Roman Catholic Church was a true church. The focus shifted from an emphasis on institution to a vital relationship with Christ. In an effort to reclaim the emphasis of union with Christ, the Baptists along with the Reformers began to point to the right preaching of the Word of God and the right administration of the ordinances as evidences of a genuine church of God. In addition, Baptist concern for church purity gave rise to the right administration of church discipline as a mark of a true church.

We can summarize the previous discussion as follows.

- A true church is a group of believers in Christ, united in fellowship and in the bonds of the Holy Spirit, and is set apart from the world in pursuit of holiness in worship and service.
- A true church is committed and submitted absolutely to the revelation of Jesus Christ as given by the apostles.
- A true church manifests its authenticity in the right preaching of the Word of God, the right administration of the ordinances, and the right administration of church discipline.
- A true church is the unity of all the redeemed of all the ages as will ultimately be revealed and enjoyed in the final state.

LOCAL AND UNIVERSAL CHURCH

In the New Testament the word *church* is used to refer to believers at any level, ranging from a very small group meeting in a private home to the group of all true believers in the universal church. A "house church" is called a "church" in Romans 16:5 ("greet also the church that meets in their house") and 1 Corinthians 16:19 ("Aquilla and Priscilla greet you heartily in the Lord, along with the church that meets in their house"). The church in an entire city is also called a "church" (1 Cor. 1:2; 2 Cor. 1:1; 1 Thess. 1:1). The church in a region is referred to as a "church" in Acts 9:31: "So the church throughout all Judea, Galilee, and Samaria had peace, being built up."

The church throughout the entire world can be referred to as "the church." Paul said, "Christ loved the church and gave Himself for her" (Eph. 5:25). He also said, "God has placed these in the church: first apostles, second prophets, third teachers" (1 Cor. 12:28). In this latter verse, the mention of "apostles," who were not given to any individual church, is a clear reference to the church universal.

The Baptist Faith and Message (2000) describes the church as both local ("an autonomous local congregation") and as universal ("the church . . . includes all of the redeemed of all the ages, believers from every tribe, and tongue, and people, and nation"). In most New Testament passages, the church is depicted as a local assembly of Christians who meet, worship, and minister in the name of Jesus Christ. Each local church is a tangible expression of the universal church. The concept of the universal church is biblical and important, but the reality of church life can only be experienced on the local level. The blessings, ministries, ordinances, and discipline of a church are only realized, appropriated, and practiced tangibly in a local congregation.

Although the typical use of the word *church* refers to a local assembly, it is also used in the universal sense. The church for which Jesus gave himself is bigger than a single local congregation. The concept of the universal church reminds us that our fellowship in Christ and our bond in the Spirit transcend barriers of race, geography, time, tradition, and denomination.

A COVENANT COMMUNITY

The Baptist Faith and Message (2000) states that a New Testament church is a group of believers "associated by covenant in the faith and fellowship of the gospel." Part of our Baptist ecclesiology is that a true church is a group of people joined together in voluntary covenant with God. The early Baptists believed that a church should be a group of saved people gathered from the world at large. The church exists as a group of believers united for the purpose of serving together as the people of God under the lordship of Christ.

Seventeenth-century Baptists customarily formed new congregations by "covenanting" with God and one another to walk together in the ways of Christ. The persons who were to be constituted as members of a church would write their covenant, and they would sign their names to the document at a public meeting. This act of covenanting made explicit in writing the vows and commitments made in baptism. The formal act of signing the covenant was considered the means of constituting the church. New members would be expected to affirm in writing their consent to the dictates of the covenant. Entire congregations would periodically have occasions when, as a church body, they would renew their covenant vows. Some Baptist churches would combine their covenant renewals with their observance of the Lord's Supper.[138]

Benjamin Keach, a leading seventeenth-century Baptist, used the concept of covenant in his definition of a Baptist church. Although the actual word is not used, the language used by Keach is descriptive of the idea of covenant. For Keach, a church is "a congregation of godly Christians, who at a stated assembly (being first baptized upon profession of faith) do by mutual agreement and consent give themselves up to the Lord, and one to another, according to the will of God."[139]

Covenant language varied from church to church and was often shaped by cultural and contextual factors. But certain basic concepts were quite common. The essential idea could be expressed as: "We do hereby give ourselves up to the Lord and to one another, agreeing to walk together in all the ways he makes known to us." Declarations of binding duties and obligatory behaviors would often, though not always, follow the introductory statements. Covenants were perceived as the most suitable way to remind church members of their spiritual commitments and corporate responsibilities.[140]

The idea of covenant underscores that individual believers through the act of regeneration are moved by the Spirit to unite together as a corporate whole called the church. The Baptist concept of a covenant community asserts that the church is the result of the free activity of God in the lives of individual believers. Our "association by covenant in the faith and fellowship" stands in sharp contrast with the belief that the church is an organization created by coercive governmental authority or institutional and territorial, ecclesiastical manipulation.

The idea of covenant implies that church life must be experienced in local congregations. The covenant community is by nature local—the result of a particular, visible group of believers united in confession. For Baptists, the covenant that joins believers together in the church of Jesus Christ is sealed in believer's baptism.[141]

The concept of covenant therefore points to the truth that a church is a group of people united together in their joint confession of Jesus Christ as Lord. The church consists of those called out by the preaching of the gospel to live in union with God and other believers. Because all members of a congregation confess allegiance to Christ, they are a people joined together in corporate confession of and submission to God through Christ.

This idea is expressed in the Baptist Faith and Message (2000) statement: "In such a congregation each member is responsible and accountable to Christ as Lord." Their mutual confession of Jesus as Christ also means that the believers are united to one another in fellowship and service; they are committed as disciples of Christ to one another. Christians within a covenant community mutually agree to walk together as the people of God. Each individual believer should have a sense of belonging to God and to one another.[142]

The idea of covenant extends beyond the immediate membership of a local church to address the relationship among Southern Baptist churches. Southern Baptist churches have historically related to one another in order to cooperate together in evangelistic, missionary, educational, social, and benevolent causes. This cooperative relationship is described in article XIV ("Cooperation") of the Baptist Faith and Message (2000).

> Christ's people should, as occasion requires, organize such associations and conventions as may best secure cooperation for the great objects of the Kingdom of God. Such organizations have no authority over one another or over the churches. They are voluntary and advisory bodies designed to elicit, combine, and direct the energies of our people in the most effective manner. Members of New Testament

churches should cooperate with one another in carrying forward the missionary, educational, and benevolent ministries for the extension of Christ's Kingdom. Christian unity in the New Testament sense is spiritual harmony and voluntary cooperation for common ends by various groups of Christ's people. Cooperation is desirable between the various Christian denominations, when the end to be attained is itself justified, and when such cooperation involves no violation of conscience or compromise of loyalty to Christ and his Word as revealed in the New Testament.

Baptist churches or mission points/efforts that are Southern Baptist are recognized to be in association with, cooperation with, and of like faith and order with other Southern Baptist churches, associations, or conventions.

Whether a church is a new work or an existing, well-established congregation, each Baptist church should have a covenant. Church covenants are usually written, and each person must agree to the covenant as a condition of membership in a local congregation. Covenants are based on and must reflect biblical principles. Although they may state the various beliefs of the congregation, the covenant of a Baptist church must affirm three things: the lordship of Jesus Christ over the church and its members; the divine inspiration, inerrancy, and authority of the Bible; and the membership of the church consisting only of regenerate persons who have professed their faith as believers in Christ.[143]

OFFICES OF THE CHURCH

Baptist ecclesiology has historically affirmed two scriptural officers of a New Testament church—pastors and deacons.

PASTOR/ELDER/OVERSEER

The words *pastor, elder,* and *overseer* are used in the New Testament to describe the same office (see Acts 20:17–31, where the terms are used interchangeably). The concept of *elder* focuses more on the character of the man whereas the term *overseer* emphasizes the function. These two terms came to be used interchangeably as they both referred to the leaders of the congregation. The Greek word *presbuteros* conveys the idea of a wise, mature leader who is honored and respected by those of the community by virtue of the integrity of his life. The Greek word *episkopos* looks more to the work of the individual whose duty it is to provide "oversight" over the congregation.[144]

Daniel Akin identifies eight functions given in the New Testament for the office of pastor or elder.

First, the pastor has overall responsibility for the oversight and direction of the church (1 Pet. 5:2; Heb. 13:17).

Second, the pastor is responsible to seek in all matters the mind of Christ (who is the Head of the church) through the guidance of the Holy Spirit and the Word of God (Eph. 1:22; Col. 1:18; 1 Pet. 5:2).

Third, the pastor must be apt to teach, able to exhort the church in sound doctrine, and ready to refute those who contradict the truth (Eph. 4:11; 1 Tim. 3:2; Titus 1:9).

Fourth, the pastor shall provide instruction for the maintenance of healthy relationships within the church (Gal. 6:1; 1 Thess. 5:12; 2 Thess. 3:14–15).

Fifth, the pastor shall exercise at least general oversight of the financial matters of the church (Acts 11:29–30).

Sixth, the pastor should lead (with appropriate congregational input) in the appointing of deacons as necessary to accomplish the mission of the church (Acts 6:1–6).

Seventh, the pastor is to lead by *example* (Heb. 13:7; 1 Pet. 5:2–3).

Finally, the pastor is to lead in the exercise of church discipline (Gal. 6:1), but not to the exclusion of the entire body when warranted (Matt. 18; 1 Cor. 5; 2 Cor. 2).[145]

DEACONS

Deacons have played a significant role in Baptist churches throughout their existence. Early American Baptists identified three "tables" of service for deacons. They were to care for the table of the Lord's Supper, a ministry of administration over the ordinance. Deacons were also charged with the table for the poor, a ministry of benevolence and mercy. Finally, deacons were to exercise care for the table of the pastor, referring to their support and service in some aspects of pastoral ministry.[146]

The office of deacon is not one of rule but of service, both to the physical and spiritual needs of the congregation. Just as the Lord became a "servant" (*diakonon*) (Rom. 15:8; see also Matt. 20:28; Mark 10:45; John 13:1–17), so also deacons are to serve the congregation under the supervision of the pastor. Diaconal service should enable the pastor to devote himself to prayer for the congregation and to oversight of the ministry of the Word (Acts 6:4). Deacons are to discharge their duties to the spiritual and material needs of the congregation and, as service permits, to the spiritual and material needs of the world.

Inferences drawn from the qualifications for deacons (1 Tim. 3:8–13) suggest that deacons could have some oversight for the church's finances and other administrative-related responsibilities. In general, the office of deacon is one of "sympathy and service," after the example of the Lord Jesus, especially in their helping one another in time of need.

The Baptist Faith and Message (2000) leaves open the issue of whether women can serve as deaconesses in SBC churches. My own opinion is that, if a local church ordains its deacons, then women cannot serve in this capacity. In SBC life, ordination carries with it implications of authority and oversight, and I believe the Bible relegates authority and over-sight to men (1 Tim. 2:12–15). If a church, however, does not ordain its deacons, then the authority-oversight prohibitions would not apply. In that case, the generic meaning of the term *deacon* (*diakonos*) is that of a servant or a table waiter. Thus, any member of the congregation could be qualified to serve. Since there is no clear instance recorded in Scripture of the presence of female deacons, I will use masculine language in my references to deacons.[147]

FUNCTION VERSUS OFFICE

Are "pastor" and "deacon" offices of the church that are mandated by the New Testament, or are "oversight" and "serv-ice" functions that a church is simply required to perform? To ask the question another way, can a group of believers be a "church" without the presence of "pastor" and "deacon"? Does the New Testament require that a local church have a pastor and deacons?

Churches must ensure that their ministries are biblically faithful and appropriately functional. Certain scriptural passages indicate, however, that having the right person to perform those duties is equally significant. For example, in Acts 13:1–3, the Holy Spirit led the believers at Antioch to set apart Barnabas and Saul for a particular mission. This passage indicates that God had a unique calling for these two men; not just anyone would do. Only Saul and Barnabas were consecrated by the Spirit for the particular task. If function were the only consideration, then the matter of who would perform the particular ministry would be inconsequential.

Yet these verses suggest that God called Barnabas and Saul because they were the most suitable and appropriately gifted for the task at hand. In addition, the church at Antioch affirmed the call of these two men by the laying on of hands, publicly recognizing the Spirit's missionary call of these men. The emphasis in Acts 13 is on the ministry need as well as on those who are uniquely called and qualified to fulfill the particular ministry.

The passages that list the qualifications for overseers (1 Tim. 3:1–7; Titus 1:5–9) and for deacons (1 Tim. 3:8–13) are even clearer. Paul's discussion focuses on qualifications for overseers and deacons, not on their duties. Although Paul does mention that the overseer must be able to teach, he does not give a list of responsibilities; these must be inferred from the names of the offices, the qualifications themselves, and other passages of Scripture (cf. 1 Tim. 5:17).[148] The list of qualifications indicates that certain individuals would be qualified to serve and others would not.

Paul places as much importance on the quality of character as he does on the nature of the duty. If the emphasis was only on function, qualifications would be of secondary importance; the point would be getting the job done, not the character of the man who performs the duty. These and similar passages (cf. Acts 6:3–6) suggest, however, that certain ministries of a church can be performed only by those who meet the biblical qualifications. If no qualified, God-called men were found to serve as overseer or deacon, the implication is that these duties would be left unattended. A person who attempts to serve as overseer or deacon and does not meet the biblical qualifications is disobedient to the Word of God.

Ministry-function is not the only concern for the ministry of a church; the right man to perform the duties is equally important. These considerations indicate that pastor and deacon are not simply "teaching and serving" functions but rather offices that require qualified men to serve in these roles.

Another issue about church officers is the matter of definition; that is, can a church be a church without these offices? Can a group of believers be regarded as a church as long as they have "teaching and serving" functions, or must they have clearly identified men serving in publicly recognized roles as pastor and deacon? Two considerations suggest that these officers are essential and definitive for a group to function as a New Testament church.

First, as the early church developed, where clear evidence exists on the subject, the Bible indicates that qualified men served as deacons (Acts 6) and overseers (Acts 20). By the time Paul wrote the Pastoral Epistles, the expectation was that elders and deacons were essential for the proper function of a church. Paul wrote to Titus in part to instruct him to "set right what was left undone and . . . to appoint elders in every town" (Titus 1:5). The well-being and vitality of the churches in Crete necessitated the right men serving in offices.

In addition, the implications of 1 Timothy 3:1–13 is that both overseer and deacon are necessary and definitive for a group of believers to function as a church and to be obedient to the instruction of God. Where the Bible speaks on the matter, qualified men perform the ministry of the Word and the ministry of service.

A second consideration is the need for order within the life of a church. A church officer is a man who has been God-called and God-equipped and who has been publicly recognized by the church to perform certain functions for the benefit of the entire church. In Baptist life, pastors and deacons are recognized as officers of a New Testament church. The men who assume these responsibilities are publicly recognized (usually by ordination) by a church as qualified to serve in these roles. Public recognition is important in order to fulfill their responsibilities in an orderly manner. If public recognition and affirmation of church officers were absent, then the congregation would not know from week to week who would fulfill or perform the duties associated with these ministries. Several people could show up on any given Sunday ready to give the sermon. Conversely, no one might come prepared to bring a message from God's Word.

Further, those who do not meet the biblical qualifications could attempt to assume these ministry responsibilities. The orderly function of a church necessitates that those men called of God to serve in these capacities be formally recognized by a church as qualified to be an overseer or a deacon. Public recognition of these offices is important because of the leadership roles attached to these duties. The people need to know and affirm who their leaders are. Certain ministries do not require public affirmation, but because of the importance and leadership biblically attached to pastor and deacon, the orderly leadership of a congregation requires the public recognition of pastor and deacon as offices of a New Testament church.[149]

The passages cited above about pastors and deacons are both descriptive *and* prescriptive. But it is incorrect to say that a church without these biblical offices is automatically invalid. The offices of pastor and deacon should be present, but situations or occasions may occur when churches may find themselves without pastors and deacons. On such occasions, these congregations can still function as a church (else why would Paul appoint or instruct others to appoint elders if there was no church, and why would the apostles appoint deacons to serve the needs of the church?). Diligent effort should be made by the congregation, however, to secure pastoral leadership and diaconal service when the offices are vacant. These offices are normative, and New Testament churches should seek as expeditiously as possible to raise up qualified men to serve in these biblically mandated roles.

MISSION OF THE CHURCH

The Baptist Faith and Message (2000) states that a Baptist church should seek "to extend the gospel to the ends of the earth" and to "make disciples of all nations" (Matt. 28:19). The task of extending the gospel (or making disciples) is achieved through *worship, proclamation* and *witness, nurture* and *education,* and *ministry.*[150] These purposes are not only for the benefit of the membership of the church but also to reach the greater community—"into all the world." The purpose of the church is to be implemented with a sense of mission according to the calling of God. Extending the gospel is the ministry of the church to the world. The declaration that Jesus Christ is the risen Savior and reigning Lord is central to all endeavors.[151]

Worship is encountering God in experiences that deepen a Christian's faith and strengthen his service and response to mission. Worship is preparatory and foundational to and inherent in the functions of proclamation and witnessing, nurturing and educating, and ministry. The worship of the triune God is not, however, just a means to an end. Worship is in itself an essential aspect of the purpose of the church.[152] The church is to worship the living God. God has appointed believers in Christ to live to "bring praise to His glory" (Eph. 1:12).

Another purpose of the church is proclamation and witness. Jesus came preaching, calling for repentance and obedience to God's kingly rule (Mark 1:14–15). One of his first acts was to call out followers who would share this mission (Mark 1:16–20). He not only taught his disciples essential truths, but he sent them out on mission to proclaim the kingdom of God and to give witness to the compassion and power of the Father (Matt. 10:5–15; Mark 6:7–13; Luke 9:1–6; 10:1–18). After his resurrection, he commissioned them to be witnesses of the good news of God's saving act of redemption through Jesus Christ, to make disciples everywhere, and to ground new converts in his teaching (Luke 24:46–48; Matt. 28:18–20; John 20:21).

The church is to communicate the gospel not only to persons nearby but also to persons wherever they are, to the uttermost part of the earth (Acts 1:8). Proclamation and witness, therefore, will carry the church beyond geographic boundaries and the members of the local church body. Implementation of Jesus' commission includes penetrating new frontiers with the gospel, acting out a belief that the field is the whole world.[153]

Nurture and education are also primary tasks of a Baptist church. Nurture and education include the process by which the church prepares persons for the acceptance of Christ and then guides their development toward the goal of Christian maturity. Believers and congregations are expected to grow in grace and knowledge toward full maturity in Christ (2 Pet. 3:18; Eph. 4:11–13). Although individuals are responsible for their Christian growth and action (2 Tim. 2:15; 2 Pet. 1:5–11), the church is enjoined to facilitate these. Church leaders have the express task of feeding the flock (John 21:15–17; 1 Pet. 5:2; Acts 20:28). The pastor-teacher has heavy responsibility for equipping the saints for ministry (Eph. 4:11–13).

Nurture and education are two sides of one coin. Nurture is the sum of experiences that nourish, modify, and develop individuals within a fellowship. Education involves the means provided for growth in knowledge, wisdom, moral righteousness, and performance. Nurture and education are concerned for the development of competent, fully grown Christians who can share in the missional purposes of the church.[154]

A final purpose of the church is ministry. The church receives its ministry from Jesus Christ. He is always the example of sacrificial, self-giving love. He "went about doing good" (Acts 10:38), ministering to human needs, challenging abuses of power, instructing his followers to forget themselves and give themselves in gracious service to others (Matt. 20:25–28; John 13:15). The ministry to which Christ calls his followers takes many forms (Matt. 25:34–40), but its is distinctive because it is done in his name and for his glory. The ministry of God's people (*diakonia*) is always by the mercy of God (2 Cor. 4:1), and it must reflect the spirit of Christ.[155]

Every believer is called and equipped by God to share in the ministry of the church. The believer's ministry involves an understanding of calling, vocation, giftedness, and the importance of daily work. Each person's ministry involves practical acts—Christians helping Christians who are in need. It also involves the church, individually and collectively, in doing good to all persons (Gal. 6:10), both through direct efforts and through cooperative efforts with other churches.

Following Jesus' example, a church seeks to minister to the whole person. This means a concern for the spiritual, mental, emotional, and physical welfare of people, both within and without the church (Acts 3:6; 6:1–6; 16:16–18; 19:11–12; Rom. 15:25–27). "Faith working through love" makes us "serve one another" (Gal. 5:6, 13). This spirit in us leads to "good works and acts of charity" (Acts 9:36). True ministry in Christ's name calls for positive action, not just verbal exercises (James 2:14–17).[156]

These ecclesiological purposes are to be a regular part of the life and practice of a local Baptist church. The regular activities of a church should include (1) the worship of God, involving prayer, hymns and spiritual songs, the reading of Scripture, the preaching of Scripture, and the observance of baptism and the Lord's Supper; (2) the edification of believers through corporate worship, regular preaching and teaching of Scripture, and varieties of service through which the commandments of Christ are fulfilled and the gifts of church members are exercised; and (3) the evangelization of the lost and missional outreach to establish churches and build up believers around the world in cooperation with like-minded churches.[157]

All endeavors of a Baptist church can be broadly categorized under one or more of these missional tasks. Each of these purposes is equally important and necessary. The task of a Baptist church is to keep these in balance in accordance with the scriptural emphases placed upon each ministry and in accordance with the gifting of the Holy Spirit for each local church.

Chapter 7

THE ORDINANCES OF A BAPTIST CHURCH

B aptists have historically practiced two religious observances: baptism and the Lord's Supper. Church history
reveals much controversy and misunderstanding about these
practices. Both of these rites are clearly commanded by the
Lord and are therefore a vital part of the life and mission of
the church. As Baptists, we typically use the term *ordinance*
when we speak of these rites of our faith. Other Christian
denominations also have religious rituals and commonly designate these as *sacraments*.

Evidence does exist that a few Baptists on occasion have
used the term *sacrament*, but the vast majority of Baptists
commonly use the word *ordinance* to refer to baptism or the
Lord's Supper. The words *sacrament* and *ordinance* are some-
times used interchangeably. Since neither of these terms is
actually used in the Scriptures for these religious rites, the
meaning is often determined by those who use them.

The term *sacrament* is derived from the Latin *sacramentum* and was originally used of a soldier's oath of faithfulness and obedience to his commanding officer. The Latin Vulgate used the term to translate the Greek word *mustērion* ("mystery"). This translation thus weds the word *sacrament* with the rites of baptism and the Lord's Supper. The concept of sacrament was eventually applied to anything considered sacred and consecrated or secret and mysterious.

The theological meaning of the term developed as the church struggled to determine the meaning and power of rituals in the life of a Christian. Initially the word *sacrament* was applied to the doctrines of the Christian faith as well as symbolic rites, but the term came to refer exclusively to those rites specifically charged by the Lord to the church. By the Middle Ages, the common belief was that the sacraments were able to draw the participant into the sphere of divine grace (as suggested in the Augustinian dictum: a sacrament is "the visible form of an invisible grace") and were considered efficacious regardless of the spiritual condition of the recipient or the clergy who administered the rite.

The Roman Catholic Church asserted that its priests had the power to convert the bread and wine of the Communion service into the actual body and blood of Christ. During the Protestant Reformation, Martin Luther and others called into question this belief when they declared that faith was necessary for the effective operation of any sacrament. Later reactions to the "magical" understanding of the Middle Ages led to rejection of the idea of the sacramental conveyance of grace.

During the Reformation, many Protestants began to use the word *ordinance* to refer to ecclesiastical rites. The word comes from the Latin *ordo* and means "a row, an order." An ordinance is a practice established by Jesus Christ that commemorates and symbolizes some aspect of his atoning sacrifice or redeeming work. The church is to observe only those rituals that can clearly be shown to have been ordained by Christ in the New Testament.

An ordinance differs from a sacrament in that the latter is believed to bring the participant somehow within the sphere of grace. Ordinances do not convey grace but are symbols signifying deeper spiritual truths. Most Baptists believe that the New Testament prescribes two ordinances: baptism and the Lord's Supper. Baptists hold to a commemorative and symbolic view of both ordinances.[158]

BELIEVER'S BAPTISM: THE INITIATORY RITE

Baptists believe that baptism outwardly signifies the inward, saving action of God in the life of a believer. Baptism is the rite in which a believer publicly professes his personal faith in Christ. Baptists regard baptism as the initiatory rite into the membership of the church.

BIBLICAL FOUNDATIONS FOR THE PRACTICE OF BAPTISM

The act of baptism certainly finds precedent in the baptism of John the Baptist and Jewish proselyte baptism. Christian baptism was not understood, however, as the mere continuation or conflation of these baptisms. Christian baptism was a different baptism (Acts 19:3–5). Jewish proselyte baptism was performed to achieve ritual purity in accordance with the law. The baptism of John was performed for repentance of sin and in anticipation of the coming Messiah. Although notions of purification and repentance are present in Christian baptism, baptism in the name of Jesus carried new meaning. "The coming of Christ was the fulfillment of God's promised salvation, and Christian baptism indicates participation in this completed salvation through faith in Christ."[159]

Jesus Christ commanded his disciples to practice baptism as part of their fulfillment of the Great Commission: "Go, therefore, and make disciples of all nations, baptizing them in the name of the Father and of the Son and of the Holy Spirit" (Matt. 28:19). Baptizing was a concomitant of the command to make disciples, as was teaching (Matt. 28:20). Christian baptism, along with the proclamation of the gospel, was established by Christ himself. His statement, "I am with you always, to the end of the age" (Matt. 28:20), indicated that the church would continue in existence after the deaths of the apostles. "The apostles did not live to the end of the age, but the church will exist until the Lord comes for her."[160] The command to make disciples, to baptize, and to teach is therefore binding on the entire church through the ages until the Lord returns.

Baptism was universally practiced in the early church. In his Pentecost sermon, Peter declared, "Repent . . . and be baptized, each of you, in the name of Jesus the Messiah for the forgiveness of your sins" (Acts 2:38). From this point onward in redemptive history, consistent testimony is given to the regular practice of baptism in the churches (Acts 8:12, 36–38; 9:18; 10:47; 16:14–15, 33; 18:8; 19:5). Gospel preaching was so closely connected to baptism that F. F. Bruce could state that "the idea of an unbaptized Christian is simply not entertained in the N.T."[161]

The proclamation of the gospel by the disciples culminated in a decision that ended in baptism. It should be noted that baptism in the New Testament was always subordinated to the gospel. The gospel of Jesus Christ infused meaning into the act of baptism; thus, for Christian baptism to precede the proclamation of the gospel and the decision of the individual to repent and believe in Christ would have made no sense.[162]

THE MEANING OF BAPTISM

Baptism in the New Testament signifies three broad realities. The act of baptism symbolizes for the believer: (1) union with Christ; (2) that he is united with Christ's church; and (3) the sealing of the covenant with God.

Union with Jesus Christ. Christian baptism is foremost an act of the believer in which he identifies with Jesus Christ. Baptism is performed in his name (Matt. 28:19; Acts 2:38) (as well as of the Father and the Spirit) and signifies submission and ownership. Baptism is thus the rite by which believers declare publicly their submission to Christ and proclaim openly that they have completely surrendered to his lordship. Baptism is the occasion when an individual who has been an enemy of Christ makes public "his final surrender."[163]

Baptism also identifies the believer with the powerful, saving work of Jesus Christ (i.e., his death and resurrection, Rom. 6:3–4). As a declaration of the gospel, baptism proclaims that Jesus died and was resurrected. The atonement of Christ is the means through which God is united to the believer. Through this union with him, the believer dies to the old life and becomes alive to the new, resurrected life in Christ. The candidate gives public testimony to the reality of this personal union with Christ in the waters of baptism. Believers profess in baptism that they have experienced the salvation of God so that they have died to the old life and are now new creations in Christ (Col. 2:12).

Baptism points to the union of the believer with Christ; the person now identifies with the death and resurrection of Jesus Christ (dying to self and sin and living for Christ) in all its realities. Baptism expresses that the believer has entered into a new spiritual relationship with God. The imagery of the outward washing of the person symbolizes the purification of the believer from sin. The immersion of the individual in water also illustrates the completeness of the act of regeneration by the power of the Holy Spirit. The raising of the candidate out of the water also points to the hope of the resurrection of the body from the dead.

United with Christ's Church. To identify with Christ is to identify with his people. Our union with Christ also brings our union with his body, the church. A believer cannot be united with the Head of the body without simultaneously being united with the body. All individual believers in Christ become united into "one new man" (Eph. 2:15). The members of the body, though many, are one. "For as the body is one and has many parts, and all the parts of that body, though many, are one body" (1 Cor. 12:12; see Rom. 12:4–5). Baptism thus signifies the inclusion and union of the candidate into the body of Christ.[164]

For Baptists, Christian baptism is regarded as the "initiatory ordinance." The New Testament teaches that a church is only to be comprised of those persons whose allegiance belongs exclusively to Jesus Christ. Baptism is the divinely instituted "point of entry" into the covenant community. The baptismal act signifies publicly the transition of the individual from the old life to the new life in Christ; old allegiances are forsaken in order that new allegiances with Christ and his people may be formed. The believer gives testimony to this spiritual transition in the rite of baptism.

Interestingly, all Christian groups perceive baptism as the initiatory rite into church membership. Baptism is a declaration by the believer that he or she will stand with Christ and his people. By submitting to the public act of baptism, a person formally joins with the church in its confession that "Jesus is Lord" and expresses his intention to be considered a member of the congregation.

The biblical witness is that baptism is the public profession of a person's faith in Christ. In fact, every baptism in the Book of Acts immediately followed the confession of faith and was considered the culmination of one's decision to follow Christ. Such was the case with the Ethiopian eunuch when he asked, "What would keep me from being baptized?" (Acts 8:36) and with the household of Cornelius following the preaching of the gospel to them by Peter (Acts 10:47). The Philippian jailer likewise was baptized "right away" (Acts 16:33). "The preaching of the gospel apparently contained the full proclamation of the redemptive work of Christ and the demand for a response of faith which included the commitment of life."[165]

A public decision to become a disciple of Christ was incomplete until declared in baptism. New converts were regarded immediately as church members, instructed in the things of Christ, and appropriately involved in the life of the community. The potential of "false professors in Christ," "pseudo-disciples," or unregenerate persons entering into the fellowship and harming the body did not seem to be a major concern. The early church addressed such matters as they arose through the exercise of strong, biblical church discipline. The modern practice of separating baptism from the beginning of the Christian life diminishes the significance and meaning of the act.

Sealing of the Covenant. Baptism also signified the sealing of the covenant between the believer and God (1 Pet. 3:21). Baptism as the "seal of the covenant" was the basis for the early Baptist understanding of the church as a covenant community. Through the act of regeneration, believers were moved by the Spirit to unite in their joint confession of Jesus as Lord. Baptism was considered the act in which this bond was established for each believer with God and his church. In the ordinance, the candidate was perceived as renouncing allegiance to Satan in order to establish a new allegiance with a new Lord. Baptism was also regarded as the "covenant seal," indicating a lifelong, public commitment to follow God and obey his Word.

THE SUBJECTS OF BAPTISM

The evidence in the New Testament clearly indicates that only believers were baptized. The consistent pattern of the New Testament practice was hearing, believing, and being baptized. At Pentecost, Peter preached the gospel, and those who "accepted his message were baptized" (Acts 2:41). When the Samaritans heard the preaching of the gospel, "they believed Philip, as he proclaimed the good news about the kingdom of God and the name of Jesus Christ, both men and women were baptized" (Acts 8:12). Upon hearing the good news of Jesus Christ from the Scriptures, the Ethiopian eunuch requested to be baptized, at which point he was instructed, "If you believe with all your heart you may" (Acts 8:37).

Additional examples of the baptism of believers in Acts include: Paul (Acts 9:18); Cornelius and those with him (Acts 10:44–48); Lydia and her household (Acts 16:14–15); the Philippian jailer and his household (Acts 16:32–33); Crispus, his household, and Corinthians with him (Acts 18:8); and the Ephesian believers (Acts 19:4–5).[166]

One of the major disputes in Christendom involves the baptism of infants. The "household" passages are typically taken as biblical evidence by those who advocate this practice. For example, in Acts 16:31–33, the mention of the baptism of the

Philippian jailer and his household is cited as evidence for the baptism of infants. Paul instructed his hearers, "Believe on the Lord Jesus, and you will be saved—you and your household" (Acts 16:31).

This verse could be construed to mean that the decision of the jailer would result in salvation for his entire household. What we know of the teaching of the Scriptures regarding the necessity of the exercise of personal faith excludes this understanding. The implication is that the jailer and those in his house must believe in order to be saved and thereby be baptized. This interpretation is validated in Acts 16:32, which says that they spoke the good news "to him along with everyone in his house." Acts 16:34 indicates that the jailer "rejoiced because he had believed God with his entire household." In Acts 18:8, Crispus and his entire household are said to believe the good news. The situation with the house of Cornelius is similar. When Peter spoke the gospel to Cornelius and his household, the Holy Spirit fell on them, and all of them began to speak in other tongues and magnify God (Acts 10:44). This activity would eliminate infants. After the Spirit fell on the new converts, Peter called for the baptism of the new believers. The implication was that only those who had previously manifested the Spirit and had glorified God would be baptized (Acts 10:47–48). Again, this would preclude infants.

The same line of reasoning applies also to the household of Lydia. The manner in which she is introduced suggests that she was either a single woman or a widow; no mention is made of small or infant children. The account of her baptism is best considered a compression of the events that happened with the Philippian jailer and Crispus.

The final household baptismal text involves Stephanas (1 Cor. 1:15–16). No description is given of those baptized, but the household of Stephanas is mentioned later in terms that can only refer to believers. These converts are called "the firstfruits of Achaia" who "have devoted themselves to serving the saints" (1 Cor. 16:15). These believers were also of such a stature that the apostle Paul instructed the Corinthians "to submit to such people" (v. 16). This language could only apply to those who were adult believers.[167]

Where mention is made of the occupants, these household passages show a consistent pattern of hearing the Word, believing, and then baptism. The clear evidence of the New Testament is that only responsible, believing persons were baptized.

The passages in the New Testament where baptism is commanded also help us in determining the proper subjects for baptism. For example, the Great Commission states: "Go, therefore, and make disciples of all nations, baptizing them in the name of the Father and of the Son and of the Holy Spirit, teaching them to observe everything I have commanded you" (Matt. 28:19–20).

As noted in Jesus' words, those who are candidates for discipleship must meet two requirements: (1) they need to be able to be baptized; and (2) they need to be able to be taught all that he has commanded. The participle "teaching" bears the same relationship to the verb "making disciples" as does "baptizing." Those who are baptized are to be taught; the basic connotation of a disciple is to be learner and follower. Infants are incapable of fulfilling the "teaching" aspect of discipleship, and as such cannot fulfill the requirement for discipleship. Infants are therefore unsuitable candidates for baptism.

Likewise in Acts 2:38–39, Peter exhorted his listeners: "Repent . . . and be baptized, each of you, in the name of Jesus the Messiah for the forgiveness of your sins, and you will receive the gift of the Holy Spirit. For the promise is for you and for your children." Some have concluded that Peter was exhorting the baptism of children in this passage.

The command to repent would determine, however, who among them were appropriate candidates for baptism. The act of repentance requires the ability to make a cognitive, volitional decision. The inability of a person to repent of sin would exclude that individual from baptism. Infants are incapable of repenting of sin and are therefore excluded as biblical candidates for baptism. The reference to "children" in this passage is probably a reference to the offspring of those present that day. The opportunity for salvation certainly belonged to those present and their descendants, but the reception of salvation would require repentance.[168]

Baptism thus signifies that a person is capable of exercising biblical faith in Christ, repenting of his own sin, and having the capacity to be an obedient, learning disciple of Christ. In addition, the ritual signifies that God has regenerated and justified the person who is the recipient of baptism. Both the divine act and the human act are realities symbolized in the ritual of Christian baptism. These realities cannot be true of those incapable of exercising their own faith in Christ. As one theologian has noted, "The union of the sign and the thing signified in New Testament baptism would seem to make the baptism of infants long before their actual faith and experience of salvation meaningless."[169]

As Baptists, we believe that we are following the biblical pattern and teaching when we practice the baptism of believers only. As we have seen, the New Testament teaches that only baptized believers were admitted into the membership of their congregations. An "unbaptized believer" is a foreign concept to the New Testament and is considered antithetical to the teachings of the Bible. "All who became members of the primitive churches were admitted by immersion; and as none were admitted but believers, none but believers were immersed."[170] "Baptism occupied an important place in the witness and practice of the New Testament church. It was regarded as the inevitable concomitant of Church member- ship, and it is unlikely that anyone was admitted into the Church's fellowship without it."[171]

Throughout our history, Baptists have opposed infant bap- tism.[172] Many a Baptist polemic has been leveled against this ritual, often identifying in strong language the problems inher- ent in its belief and practice. J. B. Jeter provides us an example of the depth of our Baptist aversion to infant baptism:

Infant baptism seems to be a harmless rite. It appeals strongly to parental affection, is invested with poetic charms, and refers for its support to a venerable antiquity, and to the number, learning, and respectability of its advocates. What harm, it is asked, can a rite so simple, appropriate, and beautiful do to the child or its parents? . . . To this system we have grave and weighty objections. It finds no countenance in the oracles of God. We read, indeed, in a book containing many excellent truths and precepts, that by baptism infants are regenerated, made members of the mystical body of Christ, and inheritors of the kingdom of heaven; but we find no such teaching in the Scriptures. The tendency of this doctrine has been, in all ages and in all countries, to obliterate the distinction between the church and the world. In almost every land where pedobaptism has enjoyed uncontrolled sway, the limits of the church and the world have been coextensive. . . . Persons [those baptized as infants] who grow up under the persuasion that they are regenerated, children of God, and inheritors of his kingdom, are laboring under a perilous delusion. They misconceive the plan of human redemption. They cherish a hope that neither Scripture nor reason can sanction.[173]

Baptists believe that a saving experience with Christ is the prerequisite for baptism. Baptism without a conscious, willful decision to follow Christ is nonsensical. Because baptism symbolizes faith, repentance, surrender, and purity, we believe that the only subjects of baptism are believers who are capable of professing their own faith. We have almost universally discounted infant baptism, believing that the practice is a violation of the teachings of the New Testament and the essence of the salvation of the individual. Baptists have understood infant baptism to rest on human tradition rather than biblical teaching. Further, if baptism is the essential profession of faith in Jesus Christ as Lord, then it cannot be administered to infants who are incapable of professing their own faith. Baptism is the first step of discipleship and is a believer's profession of faith in Jesus Christ.[174]

Baptism is thus the symbolic expression of a person's conversion. "The only question involved is the candidate's personal profession of faith in Christ, of which Baptism is intended to be the outward and visible sign. Baptism, as Baptists see it, is meant for believers and believers only, and they are convinced that the New Testament speaks with one voice on the point."[175] Contrary to popular perception, Baptists do not assert the baptism of adults; rather, Baptists contend for the baptism of believers.[176]

THE EFFECTS OF BAPTISM

Baptists advocate a commemorative, or a symbolic, view of baptism. We therefore reject any doctrinal interpretations that make baptism spiritually efficacious. In other words, we oppose any belief suggesting that baptism is the cause of regeneration, remits Adamic guilt or sin, imparts spiritual gifts, or other similar ideas. Baptism produces nothing except the blessing of being obedient to Christ.

Certain passages in the New Testament associate the effects of faith and the rite of baptism. In Acts 2:38, baptism and repentance are closely aligned. Paul stated in Acts 22:16, "Get up and be baptized, and wash away your sins by calling on His name." The apostle's statement closely links baptism and the washing away of sin. Other effects of salvation associated with baptism in the New Testament are union with Christ (Rom. 6:3–4; Gal. 3:27; Col. 2:12); the possession of the Spirit (Acts 2:38); and salvation itself (1 Pet. 3:21). Yet, in all of these passages, faith is either implicitly or explicitly stated in addition to baptism.

For example, our union with Christ is "through faith in the working of God" (Col. 2:12), and the gift of the Spirit is based on repentance and faith (Acts 2:38). Even Peter's difficult statement cannot be construed to mean that baptism saves, because he had previously stated that believers were already "born again" (1 Pet. 1:23) and that baptism does not remove the filth of sin but is "the pledge of a good conscience toward God" (1 Pet. 3:21). The New Testament pattern is repentance-belief-baptism in response to the hearing of the gospel.

Although faith and baptism are closely aligned in the New Testament, we should never interpret baptism to be the cause of faith. In every biblical example, inward, saving faith precedes baptism. The numerous instances where faith and its blessings are mentioned without reference to baptism make it impossible to advocate any belief in baptismal regeneration. Baptism is not "magical"; the water neither washes away sin nor dispenses grace. Baptism is the immersion in water of a person who is already born again and symbolizes death to sin and resurrection to a new life.[177] Baptism does not produce repentance or faith, but it does express these realities.

THE MODE OF BAPTISM

Various Christian denominations use differing modes in their practice of what they believe to be baptism. Three modes commonly found in these groups are sprinkling, pouring, and immersion. Those who practice sprinkling or pouring often suggest that the New Testament does not specify the mode of baptism. Some suggest that all methods are acceptable "as long as the fundamental idea, namely, that of purification, finds expression in the rite."[178] Contrary to this view, Baptists believe that the mode for baptism is prescribed in the New Testament. The evidence for the proper mode can be found in the meaning of the Greek word *baptizō*, the details of the events surrounding biblical baptisms, and the meaning symbolized in the rite.

All Greek lexicons unanimously agree on the primary meaning of the word for baptism. The English word *baptize* is the transliteration of the Greek word *baptizō*. The word can mean "to dip," "to dip repeatedly," "to submerge," "to immerse," "to immerge," or "to wash."[179] The term was used by secular writers to describe the sinking of a ship, drowning, and metaphorically for being completely overwhelmed.[180] Even theologians who argue for other modes of baptism (Martin

Luther, John Calvin) concede that the word intrinsically means "to immerse."

The descriptions of baptism in the New Testament suggest that baptism was by immersion. In Mark 1:5, people were baptized by John "in the Jordan River." Mark 1:10 states that when Jesus had been baptized, "He came up out of the water." The fact that John and Jesus went *into* the river and came *out of* it strongly suggests immersion, since sprinkling or pouring would not have required being near a large body of water. The Gospel of John states that John the Baptist "was baptizing in Aenon near Salim, because there was plenty of water there" (John 3:23).

After Philip shared the gospel with the Ethiopian eunuch, he requested baptism. Philip replied, "If you believe with all your heart you may" (Acts 8:37). The eunuch ordered the chariot to stop, and both he and Philip "went down into the water, and he baptized him" (Acts 8:38). After the baptism, both men "came up out of the water" (Acts 8:39). As was the case with the baptism of Jesus, this baptism occurred when Philip and the eunuch went down into a body of water. After the baptism they came up out of the body of water. Baptism by immersion is the only satisfactory explanation of these events.

The symbolism of the meaning of baptism also requires immersion. The rite of baptism signifies the submission of the believer to the lordship of Christ and the act of salvation wrought by God. Although baptism can symbolize the washing away of sin by God, the basic meaning is the putting away of sin through death to the old life and the resurrection to newness of life.

Further, the reality of the work of Christ in the life of the believer is a complete and once-for-all washing away of sin. The realities of burial and resurrection, translation from death to life, complete surrender to Christ's lordship, and the complete washing away of sin cannot be symbolized by sprinkling or pouring. Our complete identification with Christ and his salvific work requires a baptism by immersion. "Therefore we were buried with Him by baptism into death, in order that, just as Christ was raised from the dead by the glory of the Father, so we too may walk in a new way of life" (Rom. 6:4).

Baptists have always attempted to follow biblical prescriptions for the practice of baptism. We therefore contend that the rite of baptism is by immersion. The New Testament mode and meaning of baptism require immersion. No biblical evidence exists for baptism by sprinkling or pouring. To practice another mode for the ordinance of baptism would be to disobey the Bible's teachings on the manner and destroy the meaning of the rite.[181]

THE LORD'S SUPPER

The second ordinance of a Baptist church is the Lord's Supper. This rite has had various designations within Christianity, each term emphasizing some aspect of its significance. The word *Eucharist* (derived from the Greek word *eucharisteō*) emphasizes the meal as a thanksgiving celebration (Matt. 26:27; 1 Cor. 11:24). *Communion* emphasizes the fellowship shared among the participants and between them and the risen Lord. The rite is also described in the New Testament as the "breaking of bread" (Acts 2:42; 20:7) and the "Lord's table" (1 Cor. 10:21). These latter designations suggest that a meal was eaten in connection with the bread and cup after the pattern of the Last Supper. Baptists tend to prefer the phrase "the Lord's Supper." This designation links the aspects of church ordinance with the Passover meal that Jesus shared with his disciples before his death.

BIBLICAL FOUNDATIONS FOR THE LORD'S SUPPER

The Lord's Supper is a rite that Christ established for the church to practice as a commemoration of his death. On the night of his betrayal, Jesus gathered his disciples together to eat the Passover meal with him (Matt. 26:17–30; Mark 14:12–26; Luke 22:7–23). In the context of their remembrance of God's redemption of his people from Egyptian slavery, Jesus directed his disciples to his imminent death. The Passover meal and all previous sacrifices would find their fulfillment in his sacrifice. His disciples were to remember and reflect upon his perfect, final sacrifice of redemption for them.

Jesus told his disciples that whenever they observed the Lord's Supper they were to remember his sacrificial death and to anticipate a future observance together with him and all his followers. He desired that his people "remember" him during his absence; partaking of the supper would facilitate their remembrance. One Baptist theologian astutely observes, "Note that Jesus does not wait to give this rite until his postresurrection ministry but, as with baptism, even before his death He sheds 'the light of the victory over what at first still seemed to be an obscure and misunderstood reality.'"[182]

The early church followed Christ's directive and began almost immediately to observe the Lord's Supper on a regular basis (1 Cor. 11:23). The disciples began to "break bread" in fellowship (Acts 2:42, 46). Paul also broke bread on the first day of the week with the disciples at Troas. This suggests a celebration of the Communion (Acts 20:7, 11; cf. 1 Cor. 10:16). "From the earliest time of the church, therefore, the sharing of the Lord's table played a significant part in the worship and edification of God's people as they met together."[183]

THEOLOGICAL IMPLICATIONS OF THE LORD'S SUPPER

The New Testament gives clear testimony that the early Christians held the Lord's Supper in high esteem. They believed the meal contained profound implications in its meaning and observance. From the New Testament evidence, several interdependent themes emerge that are associated with and identified by the observance of the Lord's Supper.

First, the Lord's Supper is a proclamation of the gospel (1 Cor. 11:26). As was the case with baptism, this ordinance is a visual sermon that proclaims the meaning of the death of Jesus Christ. The meal is a visible proclamation of the substitutionary death of Jesus Christ. The breaking of the bread represents visually the sacrifice of Christ's body for our sake ("this is My body, which is given for you," Luke 22:19). The fruit of the vine poured out speaks visually of the shedding of the blood of Jesus for the sins of the world (Heb. 9:22; Mark 14:24). The eating and drinking of the elements of the supper are symbolic in themselves because these acts speak of the personal aspect of Christ's sacrifice—"he died for me."

The Lord's Supper is a remembrance and reenactment, recalling the sacrificial death of Jesus. Participants in the Lord's Supper are to remember Jesus, especially his sacrificial death on the cross. As the partakers "remember" what Christ has done, they also reenact in a commemorative way the events of the crucifixion. The ordinance is thus a visual retelling of the events of Jesus' earthly life, climaxing in his death. The recounting of the life and death of Christ is our obedient response to Christ's command, "Do this in remembrance of Me" (Luke 22:19). Believers ought to respond with gratitude upon their remembrance of these events from the life of Christ (the Eucharist). Believers are to thank God for the elements of the Lord's Supper of which they partake and for the sacrifice of Christ for the forgiveness of their sins.

The Lord's Supper is an event in which we declare that we have received by faith the new life that only Christ can give. Just as we must regularly eat food to sustain our physical lives, so also does the reception of the elements remind us that Christ is the source of our spiritual life. The Lord's Supper symbolizes our faith in Christ and his atoning work as the source of spiritual vitality.

Second, the eating and drinking of the elements of the Lord's Supper occurs in a context in which loyalty to Christ is contrasted with loyalty to idols (1 Cor. 10:16–21). Paul emphasized that partaking of the bread and cup constitutes a confession of allegiance to Christ and therefore demands a separation from and renunciation of all idolatrous allegiances. In this manner, the Lord's Supper becomes a repeated, personal recommitment to Jesus as Lord. The eating and drinking of the elements symbolizes this renewal as well as his life and death.

A third tenet of the Lord's Supper is communion, or fellowship. The ordinance of the Lord's Supper is an expression of the unity of the church of Christ (1 Cor. 10:17). The supper is an ordinance of the church and must be observed in a congregational context. All figuratively partake of the single body and blood of Christ. Although the church is made up of many members, it nevertheless remains one organism. Baptists believe that those who participate in the supper in a local church declare their personal and corporate union with Christ as well as their fellowship with one another. The sharing of the cup and the bread underscores that the many are one in Christ.

The Lord's Supper is also a reminder of the future return of Jesus Christ (1 Cor. 11:26). Jesus promised that he would not "drink of this fruit of the vine" until the day when he drinks it anew with his disciples in his Father's kingdom (Matt. 26:29). The ordinance thus anticipates and proclaims the Lord's second coming. The supper also proclaims that the same Lord who died, was raised, and ascended to the Father will return in triumph, blessing, and judgment.[184]

DIVINE PRESENCE AND THE LORD'S SUPPER

Although both ordinances have been the subject of heated debate during the last several centuries, the Lord's Supper has caused the most controversy among Christians. Even today, this ordinance remains the source of division within the church as a whole. The heart of the controversy swirls around the nature of Christ's presence in the celebration of the meal.

Beginning in the Middle Ages, the term *transubstantiation* was used by the Roman Catholic Church to suggest that the actual physical body of Christ was present and ingested at an observance called the Mass. The elements of the bread and wine changed (transubstantiated) into Christ's body and blood. The Protestant Reformers rejected this position, yet they differed among themselves about the correct under-standing of the presence of Christ in the observance.

Martin Luther suggested that the literal, physical presence of the risen Christ is found in, with, and under the elements. His view, known as consubstantiation, taught that while the consecrated bread and wine undergo no change of substance, the Eucharist is nevertheless the true body and blood of our Lord Jesus Christ given to Christians to eat and to drink.

John Calvin believed that Christ was uniquely present in the Eucharist, not physically (as Lutherans and Catholics believe) but spiritually. The presence of the body and blood is a dynamic in which the efficacy of Christ's sacrificial death is made effective in the believer through the partaking of the elements in faith.

Ulrich Zwingli believed that Christ's presence was not found in the elements but rather in the believing community. In contrast with the others, Zwingli believed the Lord's Supper is a memorial meal, commemorating the death of Jesus Christ. The supper should not be regarded as eating and drinking the body and blood of the Lord.

Baptists, following the Zwinglian interpretation, advocate a memorial understanding of the meal. We have consistently rejected any sacramental connotations associated with the meal. We do not believe that the meal imparts grace or is an event in which the elements are "magically" transformed. The act of eating the bread and drinking the cup signifies our faith in Christ and our reliance on his death for our salvation.

In spite of the claims of critics, a memorial understanding does not rob the meal of its meaning. The Lord's Supper is intended to remind the church of the foundation on which it rests. In this ordinance we see the mighty, redemptive acts of God in Christ Jesus. The elements of the bread and cup point to the body and blood of Christ. As visible symbols which reenact the gospel in a visible way, they remind us of the incarnation, death, burial, and resurrection of our Lord. These events signify that God through Christ has delivered us from our bondage to sin. The elements recall to us that Christ is the reason for our existence.

In looking back at the origin and events of our faith, we are reminded that Christ is the risen, living Lord. We are encouraged at the Lord's Table to remember what God has done in order to heighten our awareness of what God is continuing to do, and what he has promised he will yet do. Recalling the past in order to be reminded of our current situation and standing should not be considered as "mere" memorial.

PARTICIPANTS OF THE LORD'S SUPPER

The Lord's Supper was given to the Christian church. Thus, only believers who are a part of the body of Christ are to partake of it. In the early church, those who participated in the breaking of bread were those who "accepted his message" of the gospel (Acts 2:41). The disciples broke bread with Paul at Troas (Acts 20:7). By its very nature, the Lord's Table is set only for those who share in his salvation and actively follow him as disciples. As Baptists, we tend to restrict participation in the Lord's Supper to those Christians who have been biblically baptized and are in right fellowship with their local churches. Since the profession of faith in Christ occurs in believer's baptism, we believe that a person has not embarked on the life of a disciple until he has professed his faith in believer's baptism by immersion. Those who come to the Lord's Table must therefore have professed their faith through the rite of baptism.

Those believers who come to the Lord's Table must be in right relationship with God and with the other believers in the fellowship. Paul instructed the Corinthian church that "a man should examine himself; in this way he should eat of the bread and drink of the cup" (1 Cor. 11:28). Some people in the Corinthian church were eating the Lord's Supper without regard for whether others had food. To eat of the Lord's Table and disregard the needs of others is to partake of the meal "in an unworthy way" (1 Cor. 11:27). The person who is guilty of such actions "eats and drinks judgment on himself" (1 Cor. 11:29).

When coupled with the teachings of the Lord, this truth can be broadened in its application to include any breaches of fellowship among members of the congregation (Matt. 5:23–24). The result of these kinds of actions and attitudes is a chastening from God that could bring sickness or even death (1 Cor. 11:30). The concept of partaking of the supper in a worthy manner is not a prescription for sinlessness. The basic attitude of the believer toward God and neighbor are the primary concerns. The prohibition of unworthy participation "does not shut out the man who is a sinner and knows it to be so. . . . If the table of Christ were only for perfect people none might ever approach it. The approach is never closed to the penitent sinner. To the man who loves God and loves his fellow man the way is ever open, and his sins, though they be as scarlet, shall be white as snow."[185]

THE ORDINANCES AS THEOLOGY

The importance of our beliefs and practices of the ordinances cannot be overstated. These rites of church life embody our convictions about God, salvation, and the church. In our observances of these rituals, we express what we believe about the character and work of God the Father, God the Son, and God the Holy Spirit; the ordinances are essentially trinitarian. In addition, the ordinances declare what we believe about the atoning work of Christ and how that work is applied to our lives.

Baptism and the Lord's Supper also convey our convictions about the nature of the church, entrance into its membership, inclusion and continuation in its fellowship, and participation in its kingdom mission. The admonition to anticipate our future participation in the Lord's Supper with

Christ embodies our belief about the second coming and the nature of the final state. The ordinances therefore provide us with visible, tangible ways to express our theology about the person and nature of God, Christology, soteriology, ecclesiology, and eschatology. Baptist churches should observe the ordinances in such a way that they clearly communicate their beliefs about these convictions.

"CHRISTIAN" ORDINANCES OR "CHURCH" ORDINANCES?

Another consideration for our practice of the ordinances involves their administration. In other words, are the ordinances "Christian ordinances" or are they "church ordinances"? The former perspective would contend that any Christian, on any occasion and in any circumstance, could observe the rites of baptism and the Lord's Supper; the prerogative to practice the ordinances is left to the discretion of any believer (or group of believers). The latter perspective believes that the ordinances should fall under the administration of individual churches; the church therefore exercises oversight regarding the manner and occasion for the observance of these rites.

Although Baptists can be found on both sides of this discussion, I am of the conviction that these rituals are church ordinances. Several reasons lead me to this conclusion.

First, since baptism is the initiatory rite into the church, a local congregation must exercise the right and responsibility to oversee those admitted into its membership. The "Christian ordinance" paradigm would make credible oversight of church membership almost impossible. Baptism is both entrance into the universal church and into a local church. The "Christian ordinance" model, in my opinion, tends to emphasize the universal church aspect to the neglect of the local church.

Second, church discipline in Baptist life has historically been tied to the Lord's Supper. Only those who are in right fellowship with their local churches are invited to participate in this ordinance. Those who are subject to the disciplinary act of a local church are not to partake of the meal. Upon repentance and restoration, those who had previously been denied access to the Lord's Table may return. If any group of individuals can at any time and on any occasion observe the supper, then a scenario could develop in which a person under the disciplining arm of the church may be unwittingly allowed to come to the Lord's Table. For that matter, removing oversight of the supper from the local church could diminish the ability of a church to exercise discipline. This manner of observing the ordinances lessens the impact of church discipline.

Third, the ordinances are by nature for the church gathered. The biblical passages that clearly address the ordinances tend to be corporate. The charge of Jesus to his followers to go and make disciples of all the nations is a plural command (Matt. 28:19). His instructions to observe the supper indicate that his intention was for them to observe as a corporate group (Matt. 26:27). Jesus told his disciples to drink from the cup, "all of you." The disciples came together to break bread with Paul at Troas (Acts 20:7). Paul gave his instructions about the correct observance of the supper to the church in 1 Corinthians 11–14. Five times in this chapter the word translated "came together" is used, indicating that the supper was observed when the church was assembled for worship. Even the one apparent exception to this understanding (the baptism of the Ethiopian eunuch by Philip) can be considered an extension of the ministry of the Jerusalem church (Acts 8:1, 4–8, 36–40).

The nature and meaning of the ordinances clearly pre-scribe a corporate context for their practice. A Baptist church may, as an expression of its polity and autonomy, authorize the ordinances to be practiced or observed on occasions and in circumstances by select members in which the church is not corporately gathered. Although such practices should be unusual or extenuating, a Baptist church can sanction such occurrences. But even in these circumstances, the church is still exercising its responsible oversight of its ordinances.

DIVERSITY OF PRACTICE

Baptist churches are not uniform on the elements used in the Lord's Supper or on the frequency of its observance. Because of the strong temperance convictions in Baptist life, most Baptist churches use unfermented grape juice for the cup. Some Baptists insist that the bread be unleavened, but others use some form of leavened bread, and still others use broken crackers. Some Baptists use a single loaf of bread, from which each participant tears a piece, as a means of symbolizing their union. Certain Baptists observe the Lord's Supper monthly; other Baptist churches have the supper once a quarter.

SIGNIFICANCE OF THE ORDINANCES FOR THE CHURCH

The Lord gave the ordinances to his church for a reason. The biblical practice and regular participation in these rituals by a church brings great spiritual benefit to the congregation. These acts are significant for a church because they serve as "oaths of fidelity and obedience" (to use Zwingli's language) to Christ. Baptism provides the believer an initial opportunity to declare his or her allegiance to Christ. Subsequent participation in the Lord's Supper affords the believer repeated opportunities to renew and strengthen his personal loyalty to the Lord.

The ordinances are also significant because they provide opportunities for spiritual growth. Individual believers are encouraged in their personal faith as they witness new converts professing their faith publicly in the waters of baptism. The church is encouraged in its mission as new converts are baptized, thus bringing new members of the family of faith into the fold. As a church sees new converts being baptized, the church's resolve to evangelize will intensify. As the church comes together at the Lord's Table, corporate observance of the supper should promote unity and love among the members of the fellowship. In every way, the encouragement of faith and mission that the ordinances bring serve to strengthen the faith of the church.

The ordinances are visual proclamations of the saving deeds of the Son of God. As one preacher said, "Every Christian preaches at least two sermons in their lifetime; their baptism and their observance of the Lord's Supper." The death and resurrection of Jesus as well as our need for the new birth and Christian fellowship are declared in these rites. The ordinances are also timely reminders of what God has done and has yet to do. Our participation in these rituals requires us to reflect on the mighty saving deeds of God on our behalf. Through our remembrance, we reenact the events of the incarnation, the life and ministry of Jesus, the Last Supper, and his crucifixion, death, and resurrection.

The ordinances also require that we anticipate eagerly what God has yet to do. We look forward to our resurrected life and our celebratory meal with Christ in his kingdom in the final state.

Chapter 8

RELIGIOUS FREEDOM

Liberty of conscience and religious freedom must be included among the many unique contributions that Baptists have made to Christianity. The significance of this contribution has not gone unnoticed. When Lord Chancellor King in the seventeenth century tried to recognize John Locke as the author of religious liberty, Locke declared that "the Baptists were the first and only propounders of absolute liberty—just and true liberty, equal and impartial liberty."[186]

One distinguished American historian has noted, "The paths of Baptists were the paths of freedom."[187] Our American heritage of religious liberty "lies in the witness of Baptist churches whose devotion to this idea, through the years of persecution in Protestant Europe, makes their place a foremost one in the history of liberty."[188] The contribution of religious liberty to American life "is the glory of the Baptist heritage, more distinctive than any other characteristic of belief or practice. To this militant leadership all sects and faiths are debtors."[189]

The distinctive beliefs of Baptists that we have examined are determinative for our beliefs about individual and societal freedom. Our convictions about and commitment to biblical authority, the lordship of Christ, and the nature and practice of a New Testament church require that we advocate soul competency and religious freedom. Understood this way, religious freedom and soul competency are doctrinal corollaries of our other distinctive principles. As such, religious freedom is a theological derivative of our other distinctive beliefs, not the cause of them. Soul competency and religious freedom should therefore be construed as the application (the "outflow") of our beliefs in the lordship of Christ, biblical authority, and the doctrines of salvation and the church. When we consistently follow the logic of our distinctive principles, we are compelled to contend for liberty of conscience and religious freedom.

For Baptists, religious liberty means the ability to practice our faith without the intrusion or interference of civil governments. This sentiment is expressed in one of our earliest Baptist confessions of faith, Propositions and Conclusions Concerning True Christian Religion (1612).

> That the magistrate is not by virtue of his office
> to meddle with religion, or matters of conscience, to
> force or compel men to this or that form of religion,
> or doctrine; but to leave Christian religion free, to
> every man's conscience, and to handle only civil
> transgression (Rom. xiii), injuries and wrongs of man
> against man, in murder, adultery, theft, etc., for
> Christ only is the king, and lawgiver of the church
> and conscience (James iv.12).[190]

Soul competency and religious liberty are the two ways in which Baptists have historically understood and expressed their understanding of freedom of conscience and religion. We as Baptists have always believed that a free people in a free society is the best context for the faith and practice of Christians in a New Testament church.

SOUL COMPETENCY

Soul competency is one of our historic Baptist principles, yet it is also one of our most misunderstood theological tenets. Many Baptists equate soul competency with the doctrine of the priesthood of all believers. The popular conflation of the two concepts typically results in a line of reasoning such as this: "The priesthood of the believer (see my previous comments about this misstated concept in chapter 5) guarantees a person direct access to God without any intermediary. There is no need for a priest to communicate with God on someone else's behalf; each person is a priest for himself. One can approach God alone. I am my own priest." In one sense, each of these statements is true. As Baptists, we do believe each individual has direct, unhindered access to God. We also believe that we can approach God without a human intermediary. We further believe that each believer is a priest in service to Christ.

Two misunderstandings, however, are evident in these popular yet often misunderstood theological tenets.

First, this perspective suffers from theological confusion. The concepts of soul competency and the priesthood of all Christians are wrongly collapsed together. Soul competency addresses matters of conscience, while the priesthood of all believers is primarily a matter of mission and service. Although the two ideas are related, they are not the same.

Second, this view makes the priesthood idea a highly private, individualistic matter. The priestly concept thus stated addresses only a person's relationship and interaction with God. This interpretation is oblivious to one's relationship to the other priests within the priesthood and the attendant priestly responsibilities. We are priests who function with other priests in a priesthood. The biblical emphasis of the priesthood of all believers has more to do with service than with status.[191] To use the categories of systematic theology, soul competency is a tenet of anthropology, and the priesthood of all Christians is a tenet of ecclesiology.

Soul competency has been defined as the premise that all persons have an inalienable right of direct access to God. The heart of the concept is that man is made in God's image. In addition, the personal God is able to reveal himself to his human creation. Man was created with a capacity to know and to relate to God; thus God can communicate with and be understood by man. Soul competency requires the exclusion of any structures or intrusions that would interfere with or impede a person's ability to relate to God. In addition, soul competency stipulates that an individual must be afforded a free, uncoerced opportunity to interact with God in order to realize one's "religious destiny." When a person is quickened by the divine grace of God, he is fully "competent" or capable of responding directly to God.[192]

Baptist theologians have discussed the concept of the competency of the individual in relation to the essence of human nature. For example, W. T. Conner spoke of man's capacity for God. "If man is to live a religious life worthy of the name, he must know God, he must enter into fellowship with God. This will necessarily involve two things: revelation on God's part and a capacity on man's part to know God; or, to use the more significant expression, he must be capable of fellowship with God."[193]

Soul competency is therefore part of what it means for a human being to be created in the image of God.[194] As other Baptist theologians have noted, soul competency is a dynamic of human personhood related to our ability to think, render moral decisions, grapple with issues of immortality, and contemplate the mystery and majesty of the cosmic order.[195]

Several qualifications are necessary in order to have a biblically sound understanding of soul competency.

First, the competency of the soul in religion is a "competency under God." It is not a competency in the sense of human self-sufficiency or absolute individual autonomy. Soul competency must therefore be defined and discussed in relation to God.

Second, the concept of soul competency asserts an ability to know God. In and of itself, soul competency is not an object or idea that can be known. Soul competency is not revelation about God but rather an ability by which we can know God.

Third, Baptists have seldom advocated a view of soul competency that usurps biblical authority. In the eighteenth and nineteenth centuries, General and Particular Baptists affirmed the fact that a person's conscience could be mistaken and that Scripture was the corrective to and guide for conscience. Freedom of conscience cannot be used as a license to supplant orthodox doctrine.

Fourth, this concept cannot be fully considered independent of the effects of sin upon the individual. John Calvin provides a classical interpretation of the innate knowledge of God possessed by all persons. Calvin variously designates this knowledge as "an awareness of divinity," "the seed of religion," and "the worm of consciousness."[196] The "natural" capacity of the soul for God is the basis for the compelling, religious yearning common to all human beings.

Timothy George notes that the devastating effects of the Fall have impacted this innate knowledge of God. Apart from the gracious intervention and enablement of God, sin causes our awareness of and striving after God to issue in idolatry and self-centeredness. George further states that, in light of these anthropological and harmartiological concerns, soul competency might be better stated as "soul incompetency."[197]

Soul competency applies to all human beings, not just to Christians. Every individual is accountable to God for his relationship to him. B. H. Carroll argues for the individual responsibility of each person as a distinctive contribution of Baptists to Christian theology:

> The sole responsibility of decision and action
> rests directly upon the individual soul. Each one
> must give account of himself to God. This is the first
> principle of New Testament law—to bring each
> naked soul face to face with God. When that first
> Baptist voice broke the silence of four hundred years
> it startled the world with its appeal to individuality.
> . . . If one be responsible for himself, there must be
> no restraint or constraint of his conscience. Neither
> parent, nor government, nor church, may usurp the
> prerogative of God as Lord of the conscience.[198]

Soul competency therefore refers to the ability of an individual to approach God directly without any human intermediary. The concept of soul competency assumes that human beings are created in God's image and that God is a person who is able to reveal himself to man. God can thus communicate with a person directly and personally.

Soul Competency affirms that all persons have the "created right" of access to God. Because all persons are created in the image of God, they have the capacity to deal "competently" and directly with God. This capacity for direct access can result in a personal relationship with God through Christ. Soul competency also asserts that an individual has the ability to reject God's gracious forgiveness and mercy, thereby resulting in the person's continuing existence in the domain of sin and alienation from God. Those whose hearts are quickened by the grace of God experience the gracious presence and forgiveness of God.

When we come before God, we do so on the basis of his gracious initiative. This allows us to approach the Creator without a human intermediary. But the concept of soul competency is not the absolute rejection of the need for an intermediary. Mullins himself believed that a *divine* intermediary was necessary for the individual to know God. As believers, we approach God and relate to him on the basis of the one mediator between God and man, Jesus Christ (1 Tim. 2:5–6). Soul competency rejects the need for a *human* intermediary.

RELIGIOUS LIBERTY

Religious liberty asserts that the human, temporal realm has no authority to coerce religious commitments because God alone is sovereign over conscience. Religious freedom guarantees the right of each individual to believe as he chooses without fear of reprisal. This kind of freedom also ensures that all religious congregations have the opportunity to structure their faith and practice in accordance with their understanding of truth.

Our Baptist ancestors lived as an oppressed and persecuted group of Christians for centuries, constantly seeking relief from their tormentors. These Baptists fought for religious freedom in order to protect the right of every person to serve or reject God. They asserted that religious liberty was necessary in order to follow their conscience about religious convictions and practices without fear of external interference. These Baptists believed that a society free of governmental intrusion and state-established churches would allow them to have churches of truly regenerate members and would promote sincerity in their religious experience with God.

Baptists in America began to feel the sting of religious restrictions as early as 1679, when the First Baptist Church of Boston found its new building nailed shut the day of its first service. The persecution in New England encompassed both civil and ecclesiastical oppression.[199] The law required all dissenters (including Baptists) who refused to pay taxes for support of the Congregational Church to have their personal goods sold at public auctions, usually at a fraction of their value.

One Baptist minister, after accepting the call to serve a church, returned to retrieve his family only to be seized and thrown into prison. He was kept there until somebody paid his fine. In another incident, David Morse, a Baptist elder at the Worcester Baptist Church, had a pair of oxen taken from him for a tax of one shilling and four pence, which amounted to less than five dollars. As Isaac Backus recounts, "Such havoc did they make of their neighbors' goods, under religious pretenses!"[200]

Baptists in the southern colonies fared no better. By the 1760s Baptists in Virginia were deported, fined, beaten by mobs, jailed, and exiled. A typical example of Baptist persecution occurred in Middlesex County in August 1771.

> At a meeting which was held at Brother
> McCan's, in this county, last Saturday, while Brother
> William Webber was addressing the congregation
> from James ii., 18, there came running toward him,
> in a most furious rage, Captain James Montague, a
> magistrate of the county, followed by the parson of
> the parish and several others. . . . The magistrate and
> another took hold of Brother Webber, and dragging
> him from the stage, delivered him . . . and myself
> into custody, and commanded that we should be
> brought before him for trial. . . . To be short, I may
> inform you that we were carried before the above-
> mentioned magistrate, who . . . carried us one by one
> into a room and examined our pockets and wallets
> for fire-arms, &c., charging us with carrying on a
> meeting against the authority of the land.[201]

While some doubts exist over whether any law in Virginia allowed for the imprisonment of anyone for preaching, at least thirty Baptist preachers were incarcerated between 1768 and 1777. Those who allowed them to preach on their property were also subject to punishment.[202]

Of all dissenting groups, the Separate Baptists suffered the most. They simply refused to conform. They would not secure a license to preach, feeling that they were God called and not man called. They criticized the Anglican establishment as unspiritual and greedy. Their successful growth also sparked jealousy within the ranks of the established church. These factors, coupled with the requirement to register their meeting-houses, intensified the persecution of Separates.[203]

THE BAPTIST RESPONSE

Baptists did not sit idle and passively accept this intrusion into their faith and practice. They actively engaged those who tried to rob them of their freedom to worship according to the dictates of their conscience. They used three different strategies in colonial America to engage civil and ecclesiastical authorities. The Baptists in this country were determined to secure the rights of liberty of conscience and worship. The following analysis examines three prominent Baptist leaders in colonial America and the approaches they adopted in their struggles for religious liberty.

John Clarke. When John Clarke arrived with his wife Elizabeth in Boston Harbor in November 1637, he was a separatist, possibly hoping to find a spirit of toleration among the inhabitants of the New World. Exactly when he adopted his Calvinistic Baptist understandings is not apparent. He may have come to America already a Baptist. This supposition is supported by the fact that there is no mention of a change in his thought or of his baptism. If he had not been a Baptist, he could have been led by Roger Williams to adopt such views and could have been baptized by Mark Lukar, a prominent ruling Baptist elder. Regardless of the time and specifics of his introduction into Baptist life, "John Clarke was a Baptist of the completest and purest type, the most important American Baptist of the century under which he lived."[204]

The month of Clarke's arrival found the Massachusetts colony embroiled in controversy over Anne Hutchinson and her antinomian teachings.

> I was no sooner onshore but there appeared to me to be differences among them touching the

Covenants; and in point of evidencing a man's good estate, some pressed hard for the Covenant of works, others pressed as hard for the Covenant of grace that was established upon better promises. . . . I thought it not strange to see men differ about matters of Heaven, for I expect no less upon Earth: But to see that they were not able so to bear with each other in their different understandings and consciences as in those utmost parts of the World to live peaceably together, whereupon I moved the latter, forasmuch as the land was before us and wide enough, with the proffer of Abraham to Lot, and for peace's sake, to turn aside to the right hand or to the left. The motion was readily accepted, and I was requested with some others to seek out a place.[205]

Although distancing himself from their doctrinal teachings, Clarke did agree with the antinomians in their insistence on liberty of conscience. No longer able to abide in the theocracy of Massachusetts, he led the dissidents to seek a place where liberty of conscience would prevail.

After extensive investigation, the small band secured the approval of Roger Williams and the Plymouth magistrates to make their habitation on the island of Aquidneck, which they renamed Rhode Island. They established a democratic government that regulated civil affairs and promoted religious freedom. Clarke also founded the Baptist church of Newport some time around 1644.[206]

Another event that shaped Clarke's understanding of liberty of conscience occurred in 1651. He, John Crandall, and Obadiah Holmes paid a visit to Lynn, Massachusetts, to worship and provide Communion to an elderly Baptist believer in that town. The town officials, upon hearing of the unlawful worship service, arrested the three men, jailed them, and denied them the opportunity for self-defense. The fines of Clarke and Crandall were paid. Holmes, however, flatly refused to accept the benevolent aid. As a result, he was publicly whipped, receiving thirty lashes in Boston's Market Square. This incident created quite a stir in the surrounding communities, especially among dissenters.[207]

These factors provided the impetus for Clarke to write *Ill Newes from New England*. In this work he provided a detailed account of the ordeal at Lynn and an explanation of his views of liberty of conscience. Clarke contended that no public official could point to any Scripture for authority to pervert liberty of conscience. To restrain another's conscience violated the Golden Rule's teaching of mutual treatment. Since Christ instructed his disciples to be meek and lowly, they could not be thus and persecute others. Clarke also believed that forced worship produced hypocrites, not believers. He pointed to the parable of the wheat and tares as evidence that prohibited Christian persecution. The purpose of Christ and his authority was not to persecute but to seek and save that which was lost. He concluded by affirming that no servant of Christ has the authority or liberty to destroy the peace of an individual or nation.[208]

This work had a threefold impact. First, being published in London, it was addressed to the Long Parliament and called attention to the inequities of Puritan intolerance better than any other publication. It also allowed Clarke to make his own defense of the Baptist understanding of religious freedom, which had been prohibited in Boston. Finally, this work thrust Clarke into the role of a leading Baptist spokesman for religious liberty.

Clarke's influence as a Baptist leader and defender of truth continued to grow. When William Coddington managed to gain spurious land claims to Rhode Island, Clarke was sent to London in behalf of the colonists. After twelve years of diligent work, he returned with the land grants restored. This allowed the continuation of the "livelie experiment" that Williams had begun, preserving not only the colonial charters but also the early seedbed of religious freedom.[209]

Isaac Backus. Isaac Backus's view of the church formed his foundation of religious freedom. He advocated a regenerate church membership and church discipline, thereby establishing the self-governance of the church. The church's right to call a minister included the responsibility to support him. The state was therefore removed from supporting ministers through taxation. He also believed that God distinguished between ecclesiastical and civil governments. They were alike in that they both were governed by certain laws. They were different, however, in their organization, purpose, and legitimacy. He believed the Lord forbade either the assumption of power over the church or submission of the church to the state.[210] "All acts of executive power in the civil state are to be performed in the name of the king or state they belong to, while all our religious acts are to be done in the name of the Lord Jesus and so are to be performed heartily as to the Lord and not unto men."[211]

According to Backus, government was within God's ordained means to use the sword to carry out several purposes. He allowed the civil government to keep the peace, to protect individuals and groups, and to punish violators of others' rights. The sword could punish sins against society but never sins against God. When properly executed, government existed for the good of the people. Civil authority, however, was derived from the people and was therefore accountable to them. Ecclesiastical government, on the other hand, was to pull down Satan's strongholds, to open the eyes of the people, to win souls for Christ, to lead them into his church, and to promote faith and love in the souls of men. Its authority and nature were derived from God and his laws.[212]

Backus felt that the church was an important factor for the civil state and that Christians should be the best citizens. Christians were to submit to the state by contributing taxes and personal service for the protection of life, liberty, and property. He also felt that Christian faith was an essential good for society, since true believers were above the magistrates by faith yet willingly submitted themselves as a humble example to civil authority. Likewise, the church was not to assert itself over the state, but both entities were to strive for a "sweet harmony" between themselves, recognizing and affirming the great differences in the nature of their work.[213]

Flowing from his theory of the church and state was Backus's understanding of liberty of conscience. Among his works devoted to religious liberty and disestablishment of the state church was "An Appeal to the Public for Religious Liberty." Backus divided his work into three sections. In the first, he pointed out some of the differences between civil and ecclesiastical governments. He contended that forming a civil government and appointing officers were left to human discretion and that submission to such ordinances of men was for the Lord's sake. But in ecclesiastical affairs, men were not to be subject to the commandments of men because only God could determine what was true worship, who should minister it, and how such should be supported.[214] He further argued that civil governments are appointed to judge others and to compel them to submit to that judgment. The Lord has forbidden such in religious matters.[215]

In the second section of his work, Backus argued that liberty of conscience was deprived when civil and ecclesiastical affairs were blended together. He questioned the state's right to compel its subjects to worship upon the covenant of circumcision expressed through infant baptism. He suggested that the only evidence for such a practice was through human reasoning and not the leading of the Holy Spirit.

Backus felt that the state had added to God's requirements when the Massachusetts legislature required a minister to have an academic degree and a favorable recommendation from a majority of ministers in the county of his parish. According to Backus, the Lord has sovereignly given every man gifts to minister to his calling and does not require man's endorsement. Further, state ministers were more concerned with living in accordance with the government's laws than those that God had given. As a result, Backus felt that their most noteworthy ministers had to preach the traditions of men rather than the gospel in order to maintain their financial support.[216]

In the third section, Backus drew several conclusions from his previous arguments.

First, the very nature of the established church implied that the civil power had a right to regulate one religious sect over another.

Second, the kingdom of this world, in its assertion of civil obligation for religious taxation, sought to govern Christ's kingdom.

Third, the general assembly of Massachusetts assumed itself fit to judge other men's consciences.

Fourth, the church was to be presented to Christ as a chaste virgin. The blending of church and state tainted the chastity of the bride.

Finally, Backus stated that this practice was harmful to society since the law of Christ mandated that each person judge for himself and be persuaded of Christ's claims in his own mind. The government sought to do this for the individual.[217]

There is some question about the guiding influence on Backus's thought. Some contend that Backus, especially in his theory of compact government, followed John Locke.[218] Others suggest that he had some Lockean influence but overall demonstrated more sympathy with Roger Williams.[219] Backus's views should probably be viewed as something peculiar to himself which he developed from these and other sources.

Although sharing some similarities with Locke, especially on liberty of conscience, he moved beyond Locke by asserting the necessity and benefit of religion for society. Locke did not address the established church concept or payment of taxes for its support. Backus struggled with both. He also differed with Williams's pessimistic view of history. Backus viewed the rising America in positive terms while Williams believed that the world was in the hands of the Antichrist and that the Day of Judgment was coming soon.[220]

John Leland. Leland shared common ground with Isaac Backus in two respects. He left Congregationalism to become a Baptist. Also, while his formal education was somewhat lacking, his natural gifts and keen intellect made him an able spokesman for the cause of religious liberty. His rustic background helped him survive the rigors and dangers associated with the ministry he exercised in Virginia. During the fifteen years he spent there, Leland preached 3,009 sermons and personally baptized 1,278 persons. Leland's influence in the South was significant, especially since he spent only fifteen years of his life there.[221]

Leland's impact on the cause for religious liberty first began in his role on the general committee. In the 1786 meeting, both he and Reuben Ford were commissioned to take a memorial to the general assembly of Virginia. This document was probably composed by Leland. It made several claims on behalf of the Baptists for religious freedom. The document reminded the delegates of the promise of religious liberty, which had prompted the Baptists to swear allegiance to the Virginia government. It further contended that, despite its promise, the government's interpretation of the Virginia Bill of Rights, particularly Article XVI, greatly differed from what the Baptists believed it meant. Moreover,

> If the members of the Protestant Episcopal
> Church prefer Episcopacy to any other form of
> Government, they have an undoubted Right as free
> Citizens of the State to enjoy it. But to call in the aid
> of the Legislature to Establish it threatens the free-
> dom of Religious Liberty in its Consequences. And,
> whereas, the Incorporating Act appears to be preg-
> nant with evil and dangerous to religious Liberty,
> your Petitioners humbly remonstrate against it; and
> trust that the wisdom of you Hon. House will repeal
> the exceptionable parts of the said Act and apply the
> property to the use of the community in such a man-
> ner as you shall seem just.[222]

The general committee's most significant contribution can be seen in its influence on the United States Constitution. Leland and other Baptists were alarmed by the new Constitution. Although it did prohibit administering religious tests to applicants for federal office, it did not contain protection for religious freedom. James Madison, the Constitution's major author, found much resistance to the document's ratification, especially in New York and Virginia. Leland's opposition grew to such proportions that Madison was encouraged to visit Leland at his home. Leland sent a list of objections to be reviewed by Madison in preparation for the meeting. Two of these touched directly on the absence of protection of religious liberty.

> 1st. There is no Bill of Rights, whenever a Number of men enter into a state of Society, a Number of individual Rights must be given up to Society, but there should be a memorial for those not surrendered, otherwise every natural & domestic Right becomes alienable, which raises Tyranny at once, and this is as necessary in one Form of Government as in another.

> 10ly. What is clearest of all—Religious Liberty, is not sufficiently secured, No Religious test is Required as a qualification to fill any office under the United States, but if a Majority of Congress with the President favour one system more then another, they may oblige all others to pay to the support of their System as much as they please, and if Oppression does not ensue, it will be owing to the Mildness of Administration and not to any Constitutional defence, and if the Manners of People are so far Corrupted, that they cannot live by Republican principles, it is Very Dangerous leaving Religious Liberty at their Mercy.[223]

The actual accounts of the legendary meeting are somewhat debated. The two probably met and developed a lasting friendship. At the conclusion of that meeting, Leland threw Virginia Baptists' support to Madison, and Madison agreed to introduce amendments to the Constitution detailing the freedoms the Baptists desired.[224] Leland eventually saw his dedication bear fruit when the House of Representatives and the Senate approved the First Amendment, which prohibited the government from establishing any type of religion.

Leland's writings demonstrate a rudimentary dependence on a Jeffersonian understanding of liberty. This dependence is clearly visible in Leland's statement, "Let a man be Pagan, Turk, Jew or Christian, he is eligible to any post in that government."[225] Leland's emphasis, however, moved beyond Jefferson's understanding in its Christological motivation.

> I now call for an instance, where Jesus Christ, the
> author of his religion, or the apostles, who were
> divinely inspired, ever gave orders to, or intimated,
> that the civil powers on earth, ought to force people
> to observe the rules and doctrine of the gospel.
>
> Mahomet called in the use of the law and sword,
> to convert people to his religion; but Jesus did not—
> does not. . . . so there are many things that Jesus and
> the apostles taught, that men ought to obey, which
> yet the civil law has no concern in.[226]

Upon his return to New England, Leland joined forces with Isaac Backus to bring about the disestablishment of the Congregational Church. During this period he wrote some of his most forceful works on the separation of church and state. His most significant, *The Rights of Conscience Inalienable*, was published shortly after his return to Connecticut from Virginia.[227] In this treatise, Leland tackled the issue of whether conscience was an alienable or inalienable right. He contended that, because every person must give an account of himself to God, he should therefore seek to serve God in a way that can be best reconciled to his conscience. To surrender such accountability of conscience to man would be sinful because this is reserved to God alone. The only conscience that a person can bind is his own and not the consciences of others, not even of his children. Leland concluded that religion is a matter between God and the individual. Religious opinions are not the objects of civil government, and they do not fall under its control.[228]

Leland cited several reasons an established religion was an evil. In an establishment of religion, fallible men make their own opinions the test of orthodoxy to measure the consciences of others. Religious establishments also alienate political growth and participation, which was a detriment to the health of a society. An established religion made the church a principle and tool of the state and not of God. These two kingdoms also advocated two doctrines that were in opposition to the other. Leland felt that if the state imposed a wrong doctrine upon its subjects, it caused those subjects to sin in the kingdom of God. This was a grave evil in his eyes.[229]

One cannot underestimate the contribution of John Leland to the concept of religious liberty and its preservation in the American Constitution. Joseph Dawson remarked, "If the researchers of the world were to be asked who was most responsible for the American guaranty for religious liberty, their prompt reply would be 'James Madison'; but if James Madison might answer, he would quickly reply, 'John Leland and the Baptists.'"[230]

THREE BAPTIST MODELS OF CULTURAL ENGAGEMENT

Each generation of Baptists struggles with the best manner in which the church should relate to the prevailing culture. Many contemporary Baptists have forgotten the heritage for which our forebears fought. The sober lessons of history are ignored or forgotten. If colonial Baptists can teach us anything, surely they demonstrate that we can overcome the significant barriers that threaten our religious liberty. We must be vigilant and determined to fight for the freedom to worship according to our convictions. Each of the three Baptist figures examined represents a model on how to secure our religious liberty.

John Clarke's "livilie experiment" could be classified as a "reactionary/monastic" model. Upon his arrival in New England, Clarke was almost immediately preoccupied with leaving the area to form a separate society based on his views of religious freedom. Clarke neither attempted to transform the New England context nor to dialogue with the inhabitants. He sought to protect his own community. The pressing issues of conformity of conscience and uniformity of worship compelled him to withdraw and establish his own colony where he could implement his understanding of liberty of conscience and religious freedom. He founded a "religious freedom" monastery, withdrawn and secluded from society.

Isaac Backus employed what can be described as a "theological/ecclesiastical" model. He differed from Clarke in that, while he did react against the established church, he did not withdraw. Instead, he set out to disestablish the state church and bring a transformation of religious freedom predominantly *through the church*. Clarke was essentially free from religious persecution after his withdrawal. Backus, on the other hand, lived willingly in a hostile environment and suffered the consequences of such actions. His battles were not so much against conformity of conscience but of preference for one religious expression over another. Although the evidence is sketchy, Backus appears to have differed from Clarke in that he did not advocate religious liberty for all dissenters. He always worked with and for the Baptists, and if others benefited from his efforts, that was a secondary benefit.[231]

John Leland's distinctive method for cultural engagement can be designated as a "philosophical/socio-political" model. Clarke and Backus were hesitant to use political tactics, and they used such methods in limited measure. Leland was at home in the political arena. He associated with Madison and seemed supportive of Jefferson. He even considered running for public office. He was also willing to pledge the "Baptist" vote in an election if his candidate supported Baptist concerns. In contrast to Backus, who was content to appeal to the authorities in London and let them make the necessary changes, Leland used the political process to bring change to the establishment.

LESSONS FROM OUR PAST

Baptists today can learn much from Clarke, Backus, and Leland. First, each of them to some degree became politically active in order to accomplish their desired results. Some (Leland) were more willing than others (Backus), but they all played the "political card" when necessary. Clarke spent twelve years in England to secure and protect the land grants of Rhode Island, thereby preserving their right to religious liberty. Backus was the first to lobby civil authorities in New England. In the South, Leland became a political force who had to be reckoned with. We would do well to heed the example of our Baptist ancestors in America. Following their example, we should be politically active, engaging society and culture from our faith perspective.

Our American Baptist forebears provide us a historical precedent for political action and involvement. Some within the Baptist camp cry "foul" whenever Baptists speak too strongly of political involvement, particularly if the voice has the appearance of a collective Baptist voice. But the evidence indicates that colonial Baptists were willing to enter the political arena both individually and collectively. It is just as accurate to say that Baptists should speak as collectively in the political arena as it is to say that Baptists have always advocated for religious freedom and liberty of conscience.

Of the three models, a combination of the Backus and Leland approaches seems the most viable. We learn from Backus that the church is an instrument that God can use to confront any intrusions into matters of faith and practice. Backus also demonstrates that Baptist churches can cooperate with a collective Baptist voice to speak to moral and ethical issues without compromising ecclesiastical autonomy or principles of disestablishment. The Leland model reminds us that Baptists have been proactive in the political arena. In a sense, political activism is one way that Baptists have been able to secure our religious freedoms and the disestablishment of religion. One could even argue that our distinctive theological identity compels us as Baptists to be engaged politically for the protection of our freedom so that we can have New Testament churches.

Of the three models, the Clarke model of seclusion seems the least commendable. Granted, Clarke did use political processes to achieve freedom for his colony. In this area, we can follow his example. The concept of isolation, however, is not fulfilling our Great Commission task to engage the world with the claims of Christ. We as Baptists are free for a missional purpose. Our mission requires the engagement and interaction of our Baptist churches with society in order to fulfill our mission. Sadly, many Baptists today follow the Clarke paradigm. As long as they have what they want, they are disengaged from their culture and context.

We must note that Baptists historically have been able to serve God faithfully both in religiously free or oppressive contexts. Certain Baptists often give the impression that they would not be able to function as New Testament Christians if religious liberty should be compromised or lost. Our Baptist ancestors exemplify for us the resolve to live the Christian faith in accordance with New Testament principles, whether societal conditions are conducive to such. We would much prefer to have freedom of religion in order to follow better our convictions without undue hindrance. But when push comes to shove, we should be willing to stand our ground, defend our convictions, and suffer the consequences.

IMPLICATIONS

In 1855, a Baptist writer declared:

Of the millions of all denominations in this country, who now enjoy so perfectly as we do the inestimable blessing of religious liberty, and of all those who throughout Europe and the world are advocating it in various degrees, few are aware how much they are indebted for these views and enjoyments to the Baptists; fewer still know that this indebtedness, such as it is, is not mere accident, but a necessary consequence of their distinctive peculiarities as a denomination.[232]

Baptists have taught the necessity of religious liberty for the overall well-being of New Testament churches. The disestablishment of religion was in the best interest of the church. Further, Baptists have always believed that the disestablishment of religion was in the best interest of the church. Having no establishment was the only way they felt that free, religious exercise could be achieved. We believe that healthy churches remain separate and independent of civil authorities in matters of faith and practice.

Baptists do not believe that people should be forced "by legal enactments" to subscribe to certain religious views. We do not believe in the use of civil action to force others to adopt religious teachings. We do not believe that the role of the state is to coerce conscience. These types of acts violate our understanding of the lordship of Christ, a regenerate church membership, and salvation as a voluntary reception of the gospel of Christ.

John Broadus reminds us of the necessity of the church's remaining independent of the state. The state should in no way violate the organization, faith, worship, and discipline of the Christian church. Broadus notes that Christians should be peaceable citizens and be willing to submit to just punishments when they violate laws that are beneficial to the order and welfare of the state. The Baptist ideal of the independence of the church from the state also prevents New Testament churches from becoming dependent on the state for monetary support.[233]

Our view of religious liberty does not prevent us from participating in the government. As Christians, we are biblically mandated to be the best citizens possible (Rom. 13:1–7). We should support our civic leaders in their God-ordained duties to protect the innocent and promote the social order. We are instructed by Scripture to pray for leaders, and we should obey this biblical injunction regardless of political affiliations (1 Tim. 2:1–2). As Baptists, we have the established precedent of Baptists such as Clarke, Backus, Leland, and others to enter the political arena and contend for the biblical convictions of righteousness and justice. The Christian faith requires that we promote the values that are the essential foundation for a free society.

Our political involvement and engagement as Baptists is not, however, a union of our churches with the state. A New Testament church is founded, sustained, and promoted independently of and apart from the government. The state is not to intrude into the realm of faith and conscience. Whenever the state or state-established churches exert inappropriate influence over the religious affairs of the church, they always violate conscience. Persecution of conscientious believers in Christ inevitably follows.

As Baptists, we contend for religious freedom in order to have churches that conform to the teachings of the New Testament. Churches suffer irreparable harm when united with the state. Independence from the state ensures that the church will retain its ability to obey Christ. Churches governed by the state will not have pure, converted memberships or ministries. State-established churches lose their prophetic voice to speak when the government acts unjustly or inappropriately.

Our Baptist distinctives dictate that we strive for liberty of conscience and religious freedom. Our belief in the lordship of Christ demands that we give him alone—not the state—our ultimate allegiance. The doctrine of a regenerate church membership insists that entrance into our churches is by the new birth, not physical birth or legislative decree. Churches have the biblical responsibility to discipline their own members; we do not look to the government to enforce matters of faith or practice. We believe that church growth and the propagation of the Christian faith occur through the work and power of the Holy Spirit; we do not look to civil authorities to grow our churches.

Our congregational polity stipulates that each church should be governed and supported by its membership; the state does not hold the purse strings of the church. We look to God and his Word for the vitality and health of our churches. We believe in religious liberty because of these distinctive Baptist convictions that are taught in the New Testament.

Epilogue

OUR BAPTIST IDENTITY

FIDELITY TO OUR DISTINCTIVE IDENTITY

As Baptists, our distinctive theological identity is an expression of our loyalty to Jesus Christ and his Word. We are committed to these principles because we believe this is what the New Testament teaches. A Baptist pastor from the opening of the twentieth century, H. F. Sproles, described well the reason for our passionate commitment to our Baptist identity.

> Jesus Christ is supreme. He is sovereign, unlimited. He speaks with authority because he has . . . given Christianity its complete form. He has power to make his will imperative. His words are not counsel, entreaty, persuasion simply; but law—the author-

itative and infallible expression of personal will, sustained by appropriate sanctions and penalties.

In order to [receive] loyalty [and] obedience, a sovereign must give to his subjects an authoritative expression of his will—accessible, intelligible, practicable. Jesus Christ, our sovereign Lord, has given such expression. Not in human reason, for this has only the high and important office of ascertaining the existence and meaning of revelation. Not in Christian consciousness, for this varies with the intelligence and spirituality of the Christian community. Not in "the church," for though Romanism claims inspiration and assumes superiority to the authority of the Bible, it has not promise of exemption from error, and has given too many evidences of its fallibility. Not in individual inspiration, for the Spirit of God is given now, not to make a new revelation, but to help interpret the old, given once for all, complete without defect or redundance. But in Divine Revelation.

To us this Book is the authoritative expression of God's will. It has been and now remains inspired. . . . I am addressing myself to people who believe the Bible is the Word of God. With Baptists this Book is the only and the absolute in religion. It is a matter of no earthly interest to us, as modifying in any way our faith and practice, what ecclesiastical bodies, Romanists, or Protestants, may proclaim. The Word of God; what does it teach? We will be loyal to it.[234]

We therefore believe that our distinctive identity as Baptists as expressed in the faith and practice of our churches is an extension of our commitment to the lordship of Christ and to his Word.

We understand that some of our theological distinctives are "secondary matters" of theology. There are particular doctrines to which we passionately adhere (i.e., mode of baptism, polity) that do not essentially affect the basic tenets of the Christian faith, such as the Trinity, the deity and humanity of Christ, and salvation by grace through faith. But even these secondary matters have a certain level of importance; they reflect what we believe the New Testament teaches about the nature and practice of the church. Because of our view of Scripture, if we came to the conclusion that another view of the church was more faithful to the teachings of the New Testament, we would be constrained out of obedience to Christ to adopt the other position. We "do church" the way we do it because we believe it to be truest to the teachings of the New Testament.

LOYALTY TO OUR BELIEFS

I have discussed elsewhere the issue of the absoluteness of Baptist distinctives.[235] The relativity of Baptist distinctives is the idea that our distinctives are unique only to us when compared to other Christian denominations. The absoluteness of Baptist distinctives is the idea that Baptist distinctives are absolutely distinctive in comparison with other Christian denominations. In other words, I contend that the theological tenets that comprise our distinctive identity, as defined and interpreted by Baptists, are true only of Baptists.

The doctrinal concepts that I have argued as Baptist distinctives can be found in non-Baptist denominations. But the presence of these traits does not diminish their "baptistic" nature. Those denominations that embrace these principles can be considered "baptistic" to the degree and manner in which they affirm the concepts as we do. Many non-Baptist denominations that have adopted some of our distinctives within their confessional traditions are part of the modern evangelical movement. Many of the early organizers and participants of this movement were Baptists (Carl. F. H. Henry, Billy Graham, Edward J. Carnell, Bernard Ramm). These and other Baptists may well have infused our Baptist ideals into modern evangelicalism. Hence, many non-Baptist evangelical denominations may have inherited our Baptist distinctives because of their presence and participation in the evangelical movement.

Having said this, the evidence still convinces me that no non-Baptist denomination advocates all the theological distinctives of Baptists to the same degree and in the same manner as Baptists. Although many groups may adopt some of our distinctive theological tenets, no denomination formally affirms all of our Baptist distinctives as we Baptists do. For example, the Disciples of Christ and the Churches of Christ believe in baptism by immersion, yet these denominations do not share our understanding of the meaning and purpose of baptism. Many Bible churches advocate local church autonomy and religious freedom, but these churches do not share our views of polity and baptism. No Christian denomination therefore embraces consistently all our distinctive traits. Baptist distinctives are still distinctive only of Baptists.

In light of this, we should remain loyal to and actively seek to propagate our distinctive theological identity as an expression of our loyalty and obedience to Christ and his Word. As Baptists, we believe that an unswerving commitment to biblical authority should result in the existence of churches that are Baptist in nature and purpose. We also believe that the restoration and function of the New Testament church is part of our mission. Our conviction that our distinctives are truest to the teachings of the New Testament requires that we engage and challenge other Christians to adopt what we believe is the most biblically faithful model.

> If one is not willing to obey God in all things, does he really obey him in anything? If he obeys only in those things which are convenient and pleasant, and refuses obedience in those things which are inconvenient and unpleasant, does he not make his own convenience and taste, rather than the authority of God, the law of his spirit? . . . Loyalty to these principles on the part of Baptists is essential to their maintenance and extension. They ought to be perpetuated solely because they are of divine obligation. Jesus Christ and his inspired apostles enjoined them upon the acceptance and observance of his disciples. The fidelity of our Baptist fathers to them has modified the faith and practice of the Christian world. Yet no body of Christians will stand for them unless Baptists do. If they fail in their fidelity, then no people will remain loyal, and these fundamental principles will have no advocates. If Baptists are not loyal to them, who will be?[236]

Loyalty and obedience to Christ requires that we stand firm for our distinctively Baptist convictions. We believe that the restoration of churches that are faithful to and founded upon the New Testament will occur only through a consistent and unwavering commitment to biblical authority for faith and practice.

Our present and future vitality as Baptists requires that we remain true to our distinctive principles. Our faithfulness to our distinctive principles must arise from the conviction that we truly believe these theological tenets are the correct interpretation of New Testament teachings. The faithfulness of our Baptist ancestors to these principles has "modified the faith and practice of the Christian world."[237] Our distinctive beliefs have had and can continue to impact our world with the Word of God. Should we as Baptists fail to affirm, practice, and propagate our distinctive theological traits, no other Christian denomination will take up the cause. Our fundamental principles will have no advocates. If we as Baptists are not loyal to our distinctive traits, who will be?

We should also be loyal to our distinctive principles because, for many of us, the message and ministry of the gospel that brought us to Christ was based on these principles. The concepts of personal accountability to God, trust in Christ as Savior, and submission to him as Lord was the message that resulted in our new birth as Christians. The beliefs and practices of the churches that brought many of us to faith in Christ were sufficient then, and the same principles continue to be sufficient to change lives. Although missional methods may have unique contextual expressions, the tenets of New Testament churches remain the same.

The ability of our Baptist churches to continue in cooperative efforts requires that we remain loyal to our distinctive principles. Loyalty to our Baptist distinctives brings our Baptist churches together in cooperative ministry ventures. The continued existence of the Southern Baptist Convention, our state conventions, and our local associations hinges upon our continued fidelity to our Baptist identity. Our distinctive theological identity is the tie that binds our churches together.

We have no central governing or hierarchical body to coordinate or mandate our unity and our efforts. Despite the absence of a central governing board, no denomination in Christendom surpasses us in unity of faith and effectiveness in mission. We are able to retain the autonomy of our churches while associating together in cooperative ministry ventures because of our resolute commitment to the authority of Scripture and our distinctive theological identity that flows from it. The cohesiveness of our principles binds us together in a common devotion to our Lord, a common submission to his Word, a common passion for his kingdom, and a common conviction of the nature and purpose of his church.

As J. B. Jeter stated, "Baptists should remain united, maintain their principles firmly and charitably, pray for the divine blessing on their efforts to advance his cause, and patiently wait for their dismission from the Master's service."[238]

Our loyalty to our distinctive identity also dictates our interaction and fellowship with other Christian denominations. Christ's revealed will is our absolute and exclusive authority. Loyalty to Christ is the sole reason for our existence and effort. Our distinctive principles are in part the manner in which we as Baptists biblically express our singular devotion to him. Although we pray for unity among all believers, our loyalty to Christ means that we remain true to our distinctive convictions. If we believe that our distinctive theological identity expresses what we believe the New Testament teaches, and if we believe that these traits are expressions of our loyalty to Christ and his Word, then to abrogate or disregard our distinctive theological identity is to violate our conscience and disobey what we believe his Word teaches. We could not do otherwise and remain Baptists.

We must always ensure that we do not compromise our distinctive theological convictions on those occasions in which we as Baptists might join together with other Christians. As Baptists, we recognize that we are one part of the people of God. We should seek any and every opportunity to ally ourselves appropriately with other Christians who believe in the orthodox tenets of Christianity in the defense and spread of the righteous cause of Christ. But we must not participate in these ventures at the expense of our distinctive Baptist identity. We have an obligation to be true to our confessional tradition. We must not modify or abandon our distinctive theological traits simply for pragmatic concerns. To do so would belittle the sacrifices and labors of those who have gone before us as well as violate our own convictional ideals.

Church history vindicates our Baptist convictions. Throughout the centuries, wherever and whenever the New Testament has been read and followed consistently, Baptist churches have come into existence. Numerous accounts exist of individual Christians adopting the theological distinctives of Baptists based on their study of the New Testament (for example, Adoniram and Ann Judson and Luther Rice). Other stories relate how Baptist churches have come into existence apart from direct Baptist influence simply because believers began to follow the New Testament teachings on the church. Henry Cook, in his book *What Baptists Stand For*, recounts the story of Alberto Diaz and the first Baptist church in Cuba.

> This body of believers were desirous of forming a
> church organization, yet could not adopt that of the
> churches by which they were surrounded, or of
> which they had knowledge. They therefore betook
> themselves to a prayerful study of the New
> Testament to see if they could find the pattern of a
> church therein. As a result of such study they agreed
> upon a simple organization as they are given in the
> New Testament, without knowing that they were
> forming a Baptist church, and were afterwards much
> surprised and delighted to read that they were in

entire accord and fellowship with a great body of Christians in America and England called Baptists. The Cuban brethren had been organized into a Baptist church two years before they knew that they were Baptists.[239]

THE GENIUS OF BAPTIST DISTINCTIVES

Our distinctive theological identity is enmeshed in our doctrine of the church. Baptists have always been concerned that the church should reflect God's intentions as much as possible. The conviction that a church should rest on the authority of the New Testament and not on human tradition is what led the early Baptists to separate from other Christian denominations and form their own churches. Baptist ecclesiology is the attempt of Baptists to reflect their obedience and submission to biblical authority.

Throughout our history, Baptist churches have enjoyed both uniformity and diversity in expression. With regard to uniformity, Baptist churches normally share the theological distinctives discussed in this book. As Baptists, we share common theological convictions, and we express these common convictions in the faith and practice of our churches. With regard to diversity, each Baptist church is as unique as the individuals who constitute its membership. Differing contexts and cultures have necessitated that Baptists adapt their methodologies and ministries in ways that best fit their situation.

This is the genius of Baptist ecclesiology. The distinctive identity of Baptists is dynamic enough to engage any culture or contextual challenge in thoughtful and meaningful ways. At the same time, the distinctive identity of Baptists as expressed in their ecclesiology is stable enough to ensure that all Baptists share the common theological identity that makes them Baptist. In a paradoxical sense, all Baptist churches are alike, yet all Baptist churches are different.

I believe that our distinctive theological convictions are as needed and as relevant as ever. My prayer is that Baptists will rise to the occasion to reclaim our unique theological heritage. The vitality of our fellowship and the integrity of our message would be vastly strengthened by the consistent application of our distinctive principles to our churches. The kingdom of God requires churches that are submitted to Christ and his revealed Word. Our fulfillment of the Great Commission demands that we remain faithful to our distinctive theological identity as we seek to obey the commands of Christ in our kingdom work. As Baptists, we believe that churches which are faithful to the New Testament for faith and practice are healthy churches. We are convinced that Baptist churches are the truest expression of this ideal.

We live in a period of unparalleled opportunity and risk. The distinctive theological identity of our Baptist forebears was stable yet dynamic enough to equip these saints to meet and overcome the challenges of their day. These biblical convictions can do the same for us. The success and health of our churches require that we remain true to our distinctive theological identity. We must constantly teach and practice our Baptist distinctives. We must also be faithful to our calling to establish New Testament churches. When we are faithful to his Word, God will provide the necessary resources to achieve our mission. Our Baptist distinctives are sufficient to enable us to live effectively as obedient followers of Christ in an uncertain era.

ENDNOTES

1. Protestant scholars believe that the pronouncement of papal infallibility in the nineteenth century and the assumption of the body of Mary in the twentieth century are examples that contradict this claim.

2. S. E. Donlon, "Authority, Ecclesiastical," in *New Catholic Encyclopedia*, vol. 1 (New York: McGraw-Hill, 1967), 1115.

3. Bernard Ramm, "Baptists and Sources of Authority," *Foundations* 1 (July 1958): 7.

4. Adolf Harnack, *What Is Christianity?* trans. Thomas Bailey Saunders, intro. Rudolf Bultmann (New York: Harper, 1957); Harry Emerson Fosdick, *The Modern Use of the Bible* (New York: The Macmillan Company, 1924); Auguste Sabatier, *Religions of Authority and the Religion of the Spirit*, trans. Louise Seymour Houghton (New York: George H. Doran, 1904).

5. Emil Brunner, *The Christian Doctrine of God*, Dogmatics, vol. 1, trans. Olive Wyon (London: Lutterworth Press, 1949), 47–49.

6. Bernard Ramm, *The Pattern of Religious Authority* (Grand Rapids: Wm. B. Eerdmans, 1957), 93.

7. Millard J. Erickson, *Christian Theology*, unabridged (Grand Rapids: Baker Book House, 1991), 252–53.

8. Robert Barclay, *An Apology for the True Christian Divinity: Being an Explanation and Vindication of the Principles and Doctrines of the People Called Quakers* (Whitefield, Mont.: Kessinger Publishing, 2003).

9. Ramm, *The Pattern of Religious Authority*, 77–80.

10. Ramm, "Baptists and Sources of Authority," 10.

11. Ibid., 12.

12. Ibid., 12–13.

13. J. M. Frost, "Introduction," in *Baptist Why and Why Not* (Nashville: Sunday School Board of the Southern Baptist Convention, 1900), 12.

14. Wayne Grudem, *Systematic Theology* (Grand Rapids: Zondervan, 1994), 127.

15. Paul F. M. Zahl, "The Bishop-Led Church: The Episcopal or Anglican Polity Affirmed, Weighed, and Defended," in *Perspectives on Church Government: Five Views of Church Polity*, eds. Chad Owen Brand and R. Stanton Norman (Nashville: Broadman & Holman, 2004), 239.

16. Henry Cook, *What Baptists Stand For* (London: The Kingsgate Press, 1947), 18.

17. J. B. Gambrell, "Obligation of Baptists to Teach Their Principles," in *Baptist Principles Reset*, ed. J. B. Jeter (Richmond, Va.: Religious Herald Co., 1902; rep. Paris, Ark.: Baptist Standard Bearer, 2004), 268.

18. Cook, *What Baptists Stand For*, 15.

19. John Leadley Dagg, *Manual of Theology* (Harrison, Va.: Gano Books, 1982), 40–41.

20. T. T. Eaton, "Why the Bible and Not Other Standards," in *Baptist Why and Why Not*, 47.

21. R. Stanton Norman, *More Than Just a Name: Preserving Our Baptist Identity* (Nashville: Broadman & Holman, 2001), 164–65.

22. P. Lovene, *Distinctive Baptist Principles*, 2nd ed. (Chicago: Baptist Conference Press, 1950), 12.

23. B. H. Carroll, *Baptists and Their Doctrines; Sermons on Distinctive Baptist Principles*, comp. J. B. Cranfill (Chicago: F. H. Revell Co., 1913), 10–13.

24. Robert A. Baker, *The Baptist March in History* (Nashville: Convention Press, 1958), 3.

25. Cook, *What Baptists Stand For*, 14.

26. Gambrell, "Obligation of Baptists to Teach Their Principles," 268–69.

27. Norman, *More Than Just a Name*, 72–75.

28. Ibid., 68–70.

29. R. M. Dudley, "The Distinctive Baptist Way," in *Baptist Why and Why Not*, 28–30.

30. John D. Freeman, "The Place of Baptists in the Christian Church," in *Baptist World Congress, London, July 11–19, 1905. Authorised Record of Proceedings* (London: Baptist Union Publication Department, 1905), 23.

31. James D. Mosteller, "Basic Baptist Principles and the Contemporary Scene," *Southwestern Journal of Theology* 6 (April 1964): 62.

32. Vincent Taylor, *The Names of Jesus* (London: Macmillan, 1953), 42, 50.

33. John M. Sykes, "The Lordship of Jesus," *Review and Expositor* 49 (January 1952): 30.

34. Oscar Cullmann, *The Christology of the New Testament*, trans. Shirley C. Guthrie and Charles A. M. Hall (Philadephia: Westminster Press, 1963), 236.

35. Erickson, *Christian Theology*, 690–91.

36. Kurt Richardson, "The Lordship of Christ: The Crowning Truth of Faith," *Faith and Mission* 12 (Spring 1995): 51.

37. Norman, *More Than Just a Name*, 38–39.

38. James Leo Garrett Jr., *Systematic Theology*, vol. 1 (Grand Rapids: Wm. B. Eerdmans, 1990), 614.

39. Dagg, *Manual of Theology*, 187.

40. Garrett, *Systematic Theology*, 614–15.

41. E. Y. Mullins, *The Axioms of Religion: A New Interpretation of the Baptist Faith* (Philadelphia: American Baptist Publication Society, 1908), 128.

42. Dagg, *Manual of Theology*, 187.

43. R. W. Lyon, "Lord, Jesus as," in *Evangelical Dictionary of Theology*, ed. Walter A. Elwell (Grand Rapids: Baker Book House, 1984), 647.

44. Garrett, *Systematic Theology*, 615.

45. Thomas Armitage, *A History of the Baptists* (New York: Bryan, Taylor, & Co., 1887), 150.

46. S. F. Skevington, *The Distinctive Principle of Baptists* (n.p., 1914), 37.

47. Freeman, "The Place of Baptists in the Christian Church," 22.

48. J. B. Jeter, *Baptist Principles Reset*, 23.

49. Norman, *More Than Just a Name*, 32–34.

50. James Leo Garrett Jr., "Seeking a Regenerate Church Membership," *Southwestern Journal of Theology* 3:2 (April 1961): 26.

51. Harold S. Bender, *Conrad Grebel 1498–1526: Founder of the Swiss Brethren* (Goshen, Ind.: Mennonite Historical Society, 1950), 277.

52. Menno Simons, *The Spiritual Resurrection. A Plain Instruction from the Word of God Concerning the Spiritual Resurrection and the New or Heavenly Birth*, in *The Complete Works of Menno Simons*, trans. Leonard Verduin, ed. John C. Wenger (Scottdale, Pa.: Herald Press, 1956), 51–62.

53. Simons, *The New Birth*, in *The Complete Works of Menno Simons*, 98.

54. Dietrich Philips, *The Church of God*, in *Spiritual and Anabaptist Writers*, eds. George H. Williams and Angel M. Mergal (Philadelphia: Westminster Press, 1957), 228–60.

55. Garrett, "Seeking a Regenerate Church Membership," 28.

56. "Article XXV, 21, Somerset Confession, 1656," in *Baptist Confessions of Faith*, ed. William Lumpkin, (Valley Forge, Pa.: Judson Press, 1969), 211.

57. "Article XXVI, 2, The Assembly or Second London Confession, 1677 and 1688," in *Baptist Confessions of Faith*, 285.

58. "The New Hampshire Confession, 1833," in *Baptist Confessions of Faith*, 363–64.

59. "A Summary of Church-Discipline Shewing the Qualifications and Duties, of the Officers and Members, of a Gospel Church. By the Baptist-Association, in Charleston, South Carolina, 1774, I, 2; III, 1," in *Baptist Church Discipline*, ed. James Leo Garrett Jr. (Nashville: Broadman Press, 1962), 29, 34.

60. Ibid., III, 1.

61. Dagg, *Manual of Church Order* (Harrisonburg, Va.: Gano Books, 1982), 79.

62. A. H. Strong, *Systematic Theology* (Valley Forge, Pa.: Judson Press, 1907), 887, 890.

63. W. T. Conner, *Christian Doctrine* (Nashville: Broadman Press, 1937), 260–61.

64. Garrett, "Seeking a Regenerate Church Membership," 25–36.

65. Erickson, *Christian Theology*, 1034.

66. Gordon R. Lewis and Bruce A. Demarest, *Integrative Theology*, vol. 3 (Grand Rapids: Zondervan, 1994), 273.

67. Grudem, *Systematic Theology*, 853.

68. J. O. Rust, "Why a Converted Church Membership," in *Baptist Why and Why Not*, 222–23.

69. Ibid., 208.

70. Frederick Anderson, *Historic Baptist Principles* (Buffalo, N.Y.: American Baptist Historical Society, 1920), 21–23.

71. Carroll, *Baptists and Their Doctrines*, 22–23.

72. Alvah Hovey, "The Subjects of Baptism," in *Baptist Principles Reset*, 159–66.

73. Garrett, "Seeking a Regenerate Church Membership," 31.

74. Ibid., 32.

75. Ibid.

76. Ibid., 34.

77. Gregory A. Wills, *Democratic Religion: Freedom, Authority, and Church Discipline in the Baptist South 1785–1900* (New York: Oxford University Press, 1997), 12.

78. R. Albert Mohler, Jr., "Church Discipline: The Missing Mark," in *Polity: Biblical Arguments on How to Conduct Church Life*, ed. Mark E. Dever (Washington, DC: Center for Church Reform, 2001), 44.

79. Ibid., 48.

80. "The Belgic Confession," in *The Creeds of Christendom*, ed. Philip Schaff, rev. David S. Schaff, vol. 3 (New York: Harper and Row, 1931), 419–20.

81. "Article II, The Schleitheim Confession, 1527," in *Baptist Confessions of Faith*, 25.

82. Philips, *The Church of God*, 246–48.

83. Peter Rideman, *Account of Our Religion, Doctrine, and Faith* (Rifton, N.Y.: Plough Publishing House, 1970), 131–32.

84. Simons, "A Kind Admonition on Church Discipline" (1541), "A Clear Account of Excommunication" (1550), and "Instruction on Excommunication" (1588), in *The Complete Writings of Menno Simons*, 407–18, 455–85, 959–98.

85. "Article XIII, Short Confession of Faith in XX Articles by John Smyth," in *Baptist Confessions of Faith*, 101.

86. "Article XVII, A Declaration of Faith of English People Remaining at Amsterdam in Holland, 1611," in *Baptist Confessions of Faith*, 121.

87. "Article XLII, The London Confession, 1644," in *Baptist Confessions of Faith*, 168.

88. "A Summary of Church-Discipline, V" in *Baptist Church Discipline*, 42–45.

89. J. R. Graves, *The Lord's Supper: A Church Ordinance* (Texarkana, Ark.-Tex.: Baptist Sunday School Committee, 1928), 14, 28–30, 36–39.

90. "The Abstract of Principles of The Southern Baptist Theological Seminary," accessed at http://www.sbts.edu/aboutus/abstract.php?article=church (1858), 10/06/2004.

91. Robert Saucy, *The Church in God's Program* (Chicago: Moody Press, 1972), 120–21.

92. Ibid., 121.

93. Grudem, *Systematic Theology*, 896–97.

94. Chuck Colson, "The Church Should Mind Its Own Business," *Jubilee*, April 1984, 3.

95. Wills, "The Church: Baptists and Their Churches in the Eighteenth and Nineteenth Centuries," in *Polity: Biblical Arguments on How to Conduct Church Life*, 19–20.

96. Mohler, "Church Discipline: The Missing Mark," 53–56.

97. Dagg, *A Treatise on Church Order*, 274.

98. Wills, "The Church: Baptists and Their Churches in the Eighteenth and Nineteenth Centuries," 28.

99. For the fruit of these conversations and meetings, see Stan Norman, "Ecclesiological Guidelines to Inform Church Planters," position paper submitted to trustee board, North American Mission Board, Alpharetta, Georgia, September 2004.

100. Millard J. Erickson, "Polity," in *Concise Dictionary of Christian Theology*, rev. ed. (Wheaton, Ill.: Crossway Books, 2001).

101. Donald K. McKim, "Polity," in *Westminster Dictionary of Theological Terms* (Louisville, Ky.: Westminster John Knox Press, 1996).

102. Norman, *More Than Just a Name*, 118–19.

103. Garrett, "The Congregation-Led Church: Congregational Polity," in *Perspectives on Church Government: Five Views of Church Polity*, 176.

104. Ibid., 157.

105. Garrett, *Systematic Theology*, 586–87.

106. "Seven Guidelines for Church Planting Which Reflect Baptist Ecclesiology," theological studies division, Southwestern Baptist Theological Seminary, Ft. Worth, Texas, September 2004.

107. Anderson, *Historic Baptist Principles*, 19.

108. W. R. White, *Baptist Distinctives* (Nashville: Sunday School Board of the Southern Baptist Convention, 1946), 42.

109. Garrett, "The Congregation-Led Church," 160.

110. John A Broadus, *Commentary on the Gospel of Matthew* (Philadelphia: American Baptist Publication Society, 1886), 388.

111. D. A. Carson, *Matthew*, Expositor's Bible Commentary, vol. 8 (Grand Rapids: Zondervan, 1984), 403.

112. Mark Dever, *Nine Marks of a Healthy Church*, rev. ed. (Wheaton, Ill.: Crossway Books, 2004), 221.

113. Ibid., 222.

114. Garrett, "The Congregation-Led Church," 164.

115. Daniel Akin, "The Single-Elder Led Church: The Bible's Witness to a Congregational/Single-Elder-Led Polity," in *Perspectives on Church Government*, 30–31.

116. J. W. MacGorman, "The Discipline of the Church," in *The People of God: Essays on the Believers' Church*, eds. Paul Basden and David S. Dockery (Nashville: Broadman Press, 1991), 76.

117. David Garland, *2 Corinthians*, New American Commentary (Nashville: Broadman & Holman, 1999), 125.

118. Akin, "The Single-Elder Led Church: The Bible's Witness to a Congregational/Single-Elder-Led Polity," 33; Dever, *Nine Marks of a Healthy Church*, 223.

119. For a more detailed discussion of this point, see Norman, *More Than Just a Name*, 118–34.

120. Gambrell, "Obligation of Baptists to Teach Their Principles," 281.

121. Carroll, *Baptists and Their Doctrines*, 31–33.

122. Akin, "The Single-Elder Led Church: The Bible's Witness to a Congregational/Single-Elder-Led Polity," 37.

123. Timothy George, "The Priesthood of All Believers," in *The People of God*, 92.

124. Ibid.

125. Garrett, "The Congregation-Led Church," 186.

126. Ibid., 186–87, connects the witness of the church with congregational polity. He argues that, if believers are biblically charged to participate in the mission of the church, they should share in the decision-making processes that affect that mission. Although I would generally agree with his observations, I believe the structure of his argument is a bit tenuous.

127. Ibid., 185.

128. Akin, "The Single-Elder Led Church," 73.

129. Edmund P. Clowney, *The Church* (Downers Grove: InterVarsity Press, 1995), 202.

130. Erickson, *Christian Theology*, 1079.

131. Ibid.

132. Garrett, *Systematic Theology*, vol. 2, 587.

133. George W. McDaniel, *The People Called Baptists* (Nashville: Sunday School Board of the Southern Baptist Convention, 1919), 55–61.

134. "Elder-led" is to be distinguished from "elder-ruled," which is a form of polity that I believe transgresses the flexible bounds of congregational polity. "Elder" in this scenario is not an additional church office. The term *elder* is synonymous with the word *pastor*. The polity would thus be a plurality of pastors providing spiritual leadership and direction for a local church.

135. Norman, "Ecclesiological Guidelines to Inform Church Planters," 18–19.

136. Mullins, *The Christian Religion in Its Doctrinal Expression*, 129.

137. Garrett, *Systematic Theology*, vol. 2, 478–80.

138. Norman H. Maring and Winthrop S. Hudson, *A Baptist Manual of Polity and Practice* (Valley Forge, Pa.: Judson Press, 1963), 72.

139. Ibid.

140. Ibid., 72–73.

141. Stanley J. Grenz, *Theology for the Community of God* (Nashville: Broadman & Holman, 1994), 611–12. Although much about Grenz's theological method and constructions in this work are problematic, his observations about the importance and role of covenant for a local church are helpful and instructive.

142. Robert T. Handy, "The Philadelphia Tradition," in *Baptist Concepts of the Church*, ed. Winthrop S. Hudson (Philadelphia: Judson Press, 1959), 36.

143. "Seven Guidelines for Church Planting Which Reflect Baptist Ecclesiology," theological studies division, Southwestern Baptist Theological Seminary, Ft. Worth, Texas, September 2004.

144. Akin, "The Single-Elder Led Church: The Bible's Witness to a Congregational/Single-Elder-Led Polity," 53–54.

145. Ibid., 54–55.

146. Garrett, "The Congregation-Led Church," 188.

147. A woman named Phoebe is described in Romans 16:1 as a "servant" (*diaconos*). The use of the term is the informal designation of servant and not a formal reference to the second office of a New Testament church.

148. Thomas D. Lea and Hayne P. Griffin, Jr., *1, 2 Timothy, Titus*, in New American Commentary (Nashville: Broadman Press., 1992), 105–6.

149. Grudem, *Systematic Theology*, 905.

150. Southern Baptist Inter-agency Council, "Denominational Definition of a Church" (Nashville: Sunday School Board of the Southern Baptist Convention, 1986), 11. The following section about the purposes of a Baptist church contains excerpted summaries of this material. In this document, evangelism and missions were included in the definitions of proclamation and witness.

151. Grudem, *Systematic Theology*, 868.

152. Ibid., 867.

153. Southern Baptist Inter-agency Council, "Denominational Definition of a Church," 9.

154. Ibid., 9.

155. Ibid., 11.

156. Ibid.

157. "Seven Guidelines for Church Planting Which Reflect Baptist Ecclesiology," theological studies division, Southwestern Baptist Theological Seminary, Ft. Worth, Texas, September 2004.

158. Norman, *More Than Just a Name*, 101–2.

159. Saucy, *The Church in God's Program*, 192.

160. Ibid.

161. F. F. Bruce, *The Book of Acts*, New International Commentary Series (Grand Rapids: Wm. B. Eerdmans, 1988), 77.

162. Saucy, *The Church in God's Program*, 193.

163. G. R. Beasley-Murray, *Baptism Today and Tomorrow* (New York: Macmillan, 1966), 43.

164. Saucy, *The Church in God's Program*, 195.

165. Ibid.

166. Ibid., 199–200.

167. Ibid., 200–2.

168. Ibid., 199.

169. Ibid., 202.

170. John Quincy Adams, *Baptists the Only Thorough Religious Reformers*, rev. ed. (New York: Sheldon & Co., 1876), 152.

171. Cook, *What Baptists Stand For*, 135.

172. For an excellent yet brief history of the rise of infant baptism, see Saucy, 203–5.

173. Jeter, "Believers the Only Subjects of Baptism," in *Baptist Principles Reset*, 559–61.

174. J. B. Moody, "Why Baptism as Symbol and Not a Saving Ordinance," in *Baptist Why and Why Not*, 183–84.

175. Cook, *What Baptists Stand For*, 135.

176. Norman, *Ecclesiological Guidelines to Inform Church Planters*, 27.

177. Robert A. Baker, *The Baptist March in History* (Nashville: Convention Press, 1958), 8.

178. Louis Berkhof, *Systematic Theology*, 4th ed. (Grand Rapids: Wm. B. Eerdmans, 1939), 629.

179. Joseph H. Thayer, *A Greek-English Lexicon of the New Testament*, 4th ed. (Nashville: Broadman Press, 1977), 94; William F. Arndt and E. Wilbur Gingrich, *A Greek-English Lexicon of the New Testament and Other Early Christian Literature*, 2nd ed., rev. (Chicago: University of Chicago Press, 1979), 131; Hermann Cremer, *Biblico-Theological Lexicon of New Testament Greek*, trans. William Urwick, 4th ed. (Edinburgh: T. & T. Clark, 1895), 126; H. G. Liddell and Robert Scott, eds., *A Greek-English Lexicon*, rev. (New York: Oxford University Press, 1996), 305–6.

180. Albrecht Oepke, "*baptō, baptizō*," in *Theological Dictionary of the New Testament*, vol. 1, ed. Gerhard Kittel, trans. and ed. Geoffrey W. Bromiley (Grand Rapids: Eerdmans, 1964), 530.

181. Mullins, *The Christian Religion in Its Doctrinal Expression*, 166.

182. Saucy, *The Church in God's Program*, 215.

183. Ibid., 216.

184. Garrett, *Systematic Theology*, 611–12.

185. William Barclay, *The Letters to the Corinthians* (Philadelphia: Westminster Press, 1956), 117.

186. John Locke, *A Letter Concerning Toleration* (1689).

187. George Bancroft, *History of the United States*, vol. 1 (New York: D. Appleton and Co., 1892), 608.

188. Cecil Northcott, *Religious Liberty* (New York: Macmillan Co., 1949), 28.

189. Charles Evans Hughes, "Address of Charles E. Hughes at the Laying of the Corner-Stone of the National Baptist Memorial to Religious Liberty," *Religious Herald*, 90:4, 27 April 1922.

190. "Article 84, Propositions and Conclusions Concerning True Christian Religion, 1612–1614," in *Baptist Confessions of Faith*, 140.

191. For an excellent historical and theological explanation of the Reformation concept of the priesthood of all believers, see Timothy George, "The Priesthood of All Believers and the Quest for Theological Integrity," *Criswell Theological Review* 3 (Spring 1989): 283–94.

192. Mullins, *The Christian Religion in Its Doctrinal Expression*, 59–68.

193. Conner, *Christian Doctrine*, 17.

194. George, "The Priesthood of All Believers," 284.

195. Cf. J. P. Boyce, *Abstract of Systematic Theology* (Philadelphia: American Baptist Publication Society, 1899), 30; Alvah Hovey, *Manual of Christian Theology* (New York: Silver, Burdett, and Co., 1900), 33–40; A. H. Strong, *Systematic Theology* (Valley Forge, Pa.: Judson Press, 1907), 497–513; E. Y. Mullins, *The Christian Religion in Its Doctrinal Expression* (Valley Forge, Pa.: Judson Press, 1917), 259–60; Erickson, *Christian Theology*, 512–17; Lewis and Demarest, *Integrative Theology*, vol. 2, 142–59; Garrett, *Systematic Theology*, vol. 1, 401–3.

196. John Calvin, *Institutes of the Christian Religion*, eds. John T. McNeill and F. Lewis Battles (Philadelphia: Westminster Press, 1960), 1:3–4.

197. George, "The Priesthood of All Believers," 284–85.

198. Carroll, *Baptists and Their Doctrines*, 15, 18.

199. H. Leon McBeth, *The Baptist Heritage* (Nashville: Broadman Press, 1987), 256.

200. Isaac Backus, *A History of New England with Particular Reference to the Denomination of Christians Called Baptists*, vol. 2 (Newton, Mass.: Backus Historical Society, 1871), 94–95.

201. Robert Baylor Semple, *History and Progress of the Baptists in Virginia* (Richmond, Va.: Pitt and Dickinson, 1894), 481–82.

202. Ibid., 270–71.

203. Robert G. Torbet, *A History of the Baptists* (Valley Forge, Pa.: Judson Press, 1969), 239.

204. A. H. Newman, *A History of the Baptist Churches in the United States* (Philadelphia: American Baptist Publication Society, 1894), 96–108.

205. Ibid., 96–97.

206. Ibid., 96. Although second in date to the Baptist church at Providence, it "deserves the first place as regards the consistent and persistent

devotion of its leaders to Baptist principles, the thoroughness and vigor of its organization, and its evangelistic zeal."

207. Edwin S. Gaustad, "John Clarke: 'Good Newes from Rhode Island,'" *Baptist History and Heritage* 24 (October 1989): 22.

208. John Clarke, "Ill Newes from New England," in *Colonial Baptists: Massachusetts and Rhode Island*, ed. Edwin S. Gaustad (New York: Arno Press, 1980), 96–113.

209. Gaustad, "Good Newes from Rhode Island," 23–26.

210. Stanley Grenz, *Isaac Backus—Puritan and Baptist* (Macon, Ga.: Mercer University Press, 1983), 133; T. B. Maston, *Isaac Backus: Pioneer of Religious Liberty* (Rochester: American Baptist Historical Society, 1962), 55–59.

211. Isaac Backus, "An Appeal to the Public for Religious Liberty, 1773" in *A Sourcebook for Baptist Heritage*, ed. H. Leon McBeth (Nashville: Broadman Press, 1990), 174.

212. Ibid., 175.

213. Maston, *Isaac Backus*, 69–74.

214. Backus, "An Appeal to the Public," 174.

215. Ibid., 174–75.

216. Ibid., 175.

217. Ibid., 177.

218. Maston, *Isaac Backus*, 75–77, where he points out that Backus quoted Locke more extensively than Williams.

219. William R. Estep, *Revolution within the Revolution* (Grand Rapids: Wm. B. Eerdmans, 1990), 113, where he suggests that, in his third phase of life, Backus rediscovered Williams's Baptist traditions of religious liberty, separation of church and state, and pietism.

220. William G. McLoughlin, *Soul Liberty: The Baptists' Struggle in New England, 1630–1833* (Hanover, Mass.: Brown University Press, 1931), 258–59. Williams opposed conformity of conscience and uniformity of worship. Backus did not face that particular issue but had to contend with the preferred church that received financial aid from the state but granted little toleration to dissenters.

221. Jack Manly, "Leland, John," in *Encyclopedia of Southern Baptists*, vol. 2 (Nashville: Broadman Press, 1958), 783.

222. Garnett Ryland, *The Baptists of Virginia: 1699–1926* (Richmond: Virginia Baptist Board of Mission and Education, 1955), 130.

223. Leland, as cited in Estep, *Revolution within the Revolution*, 199–201.

224. McBeth, *The Baptist Heritage*, 282.

225. Leland, *The Writings of John Leland*, ed. L. F. Greene (New York: Arno Press, 1969), 191.

226. Ibid., 187.

227. Estep, *Revolution within the Revolution*, 158.

228. Leland, "The Rights of Conscience Inalienable, 1791," in *A Sourcebook for Baptist Heritage*, 179.

229. Ibid., 180.

230. Joseph Dawson, *Baptists and the American Republic* (Nashville: Broadman Press, 1956), 117.

231. McLoughlin, *Soul Liberty*, 255. McLoughlin further states that Backus was open to using whatever channels he could to further his cause. If engaging in military conflict aided the effort, Backus was for it. If civil disobedience could make a difference, Backus was open to it. The records do not indicate, however, that he ever actively associated with other dissenting groups, particularly the Quakers.

232. T. F. Curtis, *The Progress of Baptist Principles* (Boston: Gould and Lincoln, 1855), 19.

233. John Broadus, *The Duty of Baptists to Teach Their Distinctive Views* (Philadelphia: American Baptist Publication Society, 1881), 10.

234. H. F. Sproles, "Why Loyalty to Baptist Principles," in *Baptist Why and Why Not* (Nashville: Sunday School Board of the Southern Baptist Convention, 1900), 364–66.

235. Norman, *More Than Just a Name*, 160–62.

236. Sproles, "Why Loyalty to Baptist Principles,"367–68.

237. Ibid., 368.

238. Jeter, "Obligation of Baptists to Their Principles," 140.

239. Cook, *What Baptists Stand For,* 23–24.

SCRIPTURE INDEX

NAME INDEX

SUBJECT INDEX